The Complete Guide to Maine's Lighthouses

From Kittery to Calais

By Larry Freeman

The Complete Guide to Maine's Lighthouses. Copyright 2019 by Larry Freeman. No part of this book may be reproduced or transmitted in any form or by any means, electronic, mechanical, magnetic, photographic including photocopying, recording or by any information storage and retrieval system, without permission of the author.

Although every precaution has been taken in the preparation of this book, the author assumes no responsibility for errors or omissions.

Portions of this book refer to text contained in submissions made to the National Register of Historic Places. Due to the varying nature of these submissions, in many cases the original text is paraphrased and/or condensed. For the full, unaltered text refer to:
http://www.nps.gov/subjects/nationalregister/index.htm

In no case was any attempt made to alter the intent or facts contained within these historic documents.

Steadfast, serene, immovable, the same
Year after year, through all the silent night
Burns on forevermore that quenchless flame,
Shines on that inextinguishable light!

Henry Wadsworth Longfellow

"The Lighthouse"

***

Table of Contents

Maine's Lighthouses – by the Numbers 1
Introduction 3
1 Whaleback Light 9
2 Boon Island Light 13
3 Cape Neddick Light (The Nubble) 17
4 Goat Island Light 21
5 Wood Island Light 25
6 Cape Elizabeth Light (Two Lights) 29
7 Portland Head Light 33
8 Ram Island Ledge Light 39
9 Spring Point Ledge Light 43
10 Portland Breakwater Light (Bug Light) 47
11 Halfway Rock Light 51
12 Seguin Island Light 55
13 Pond Island Light 59
14 Perkins Island Light 61
15 Squirrel Point Light 65
16 Doubling Point Range Lights 69
17 Doubling Point Light 73
18 Hendricks Head Light 77
19 Cuckolds Light 81
20 Burnt Island Light 87
21 Ram Island Light 91
22 Pemaquid Point Light 95
23 Monhegan Island Light 99
24 Franklin Island Light 103

25 Marshall Point Light 107

26 Tenants Harbor Light (Southern Island Light) 111

27 Whitehead Light 115

28 Two Bush Island Light 119

29 Matinicus Rock Light 123

30 Owls Head Light 127

31 Rockland Breakwater Harbor Light 135

32 Rockland Southwest Harbor Light 139

33 Indian Island Light 141

34 Curtis Island Light 145

35 Grindle Point Light 149

36 Fort Point Light 153

37 Dice Head Light 157

38 Pumpkin Island Light 161

39 Eagle Island Light 165

40 Goose Rocks Light 169

41 Browns Head Light 173

42 Heron Neck Light 177

43 Saddleback Ledge Light 181

44 Isle au Haut Light (Robinson Point Light) 185

45 Deer Island Thorofare Light (Mark Island Light) 189

46 Blue Hill Bay Light 193

47 Burnt Coat Harbor Light 195

48 Bass Harbor Head Light 199

49 Great Duck Island Light 203

50 Mount Desert Rock Light 207

51 Baker Island Light 211

52 Bear Island Light 217

53 Egg Rock Light 221
54 Winter Harbor Light (Mark Island Light) 225
55 Prospect Harbor Light 229
56 Petit Manan Light 235
57 Narraguagus Light (Pond Island Light) 243
58 Nash Island Light 247
59 Moose Peak Light 251
60 Libby Island Light 255
61 Little River Light 261
62 West Quoddy Head Light 267
63 Lubec Channel Light 271
64 Whitlocks Mill Light 275
65 Ladies Delight Light 279
The Evolution and Restoration of Maine's Lighthouses 283
How Far Away Can You See a Lighthouse? 288
What's in a Light? 295
Maine Lighthouse Museums and Events 301
Lighthouse Towns and Cities in Maine 303
Maine Lighthouse Grounds Access 307
Lighthouse Cruises Mentioned in this Book 309
Mainland Lighthouse Views 315

***

The Complete Guide to Maine's Lighthouses

Maine's Lighthouses – by the Numbers

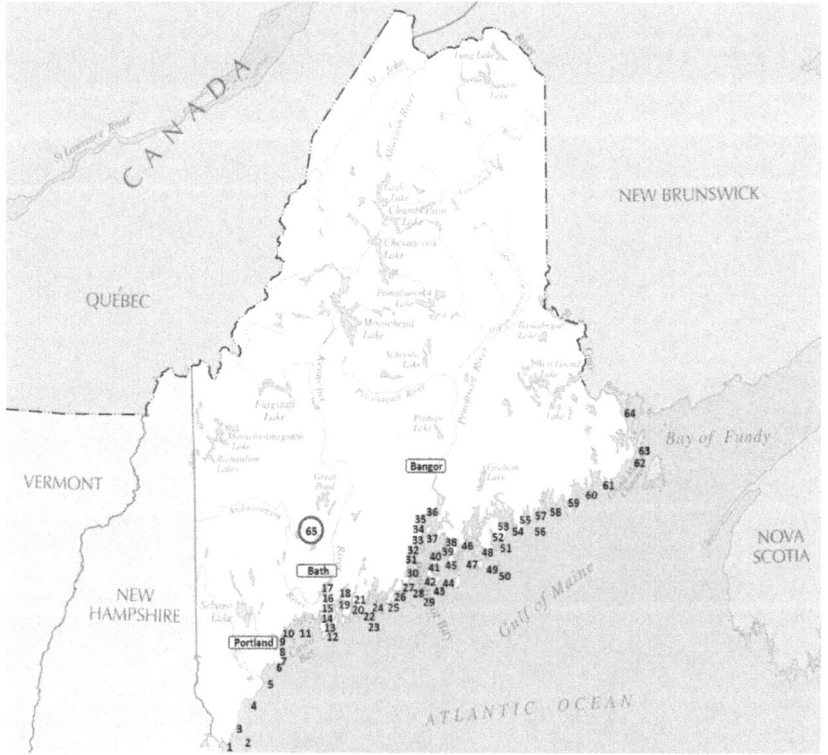

1 Whaleback Light
2 Boon Island Light
3 Cape Neddick Light
4 Goat Island Light
5 Wood Island Light
6 Cape Elizabeth Light
7 Portland Head Light
8 Ram Island Ledge Light
9 Spring Point Ledge Light
10 Portland Breakwater
11 Halfway Rock Light
12 Seguin Island Light
13 Pond Island Light
14 Perkins Island Light
15 Squirrel Point Light
16 Doubling Point Range
17 Doubling Point Light
18 Hendricks Head Light
19 Cuckolds Island Light
20 Burnt Island Light
21 Ram Island Light
22 Pemaquid Point Light

23 Monhegan Island Light
24 Franklin Island Light
25 Marshall Point Light
26 Tenants Harbor Light
27 Whitehead Light
28 Two Bush Island
29 Matinicus Rock Light
30 Owls Head Light
31 Rockland Breakwater Harbor
32 Rockland Southwest Harbor
33 Indian Island Light
34 Curtis Island Light
35 Grindle Point Light
36 Fort Point Light
37 Dice Head Light
38 Pumpkin Island Light
39 Eagle Island Light
40 Goose Rocks Light
41 Browns Head Light
42 Heron Neck Light
43 Saddleback Ledge Light
44 Isle au Haute Light

45 Deer Island Light
46 Blue Hill Bay Light
47 Burnt Coat Harbor
48 Bass Harbor Head Light
49 Great Duck Island Light
50 Mt Desert Rock island
51 Baker Island Light
52 Bear Island Light
53 Egg Rock Light
54 Winter Harbor Light
55 Prospect Harbor Light
56 Petit Manan Light
57 Narraguagus Light
58 Nash Island Light
59 Moose Peak Light
60 Libby Island Light
61 Little River Light
62 West Quoddy Head
63 Lubec Channel Light
64 Whitlocks Mill Light
65 Ladies Delight Light

***

Introduction

The coast of Maine contains 3,478 miles of tidal-influenced shoreline and 3,166 named islands, from the southern town of Kittery on the New Hampshire border to the northeastern town of Calais on the Canadian border.

Along this coastline, hundreds of lighted buoys and beacons have been installed to help guide mariners through otherwise treacherous waters. Among these beacons are a series of historical lighthouses - 64 in all, built between 1794 and 1908. From Whaleback Light at the mouth of the Piscataqua River, to Whitlock's Light on the south side of the St. Croix River, these lighthouses stand as a rugged testament of Maine's maritime history.

In addition to these coastal lighthouses, one single inland lighthouse is included, for reasons explained later – bringing the total to 65 Maine lighthouses in existence today.

In this book, the coastal lighthouses are numbered in ascending order from south to north, based on an imaginary journey along Maine's Atlantic shoreline with its many bays and inlets, from Kittery to Calais.

Maine Lighthouse Categories and Clusters

Maine's lighthouses fall in two primary categories: Those that guide vessels while within Maine's busiest harbors and rivers, and those that guide vessels while navigating along the open waters of the Atlantic coast.

Three of Maine harbors are of particular importance, as they comprise over one-half of Maine's historic light stations. These harbors include 1) the deep water port of Portland's Casco Bay, a key commerce district, 2) the shipbuilding district of Bath, where Sagadahoc Bay is fed by the Kennebec and Androscoggin Rivers, and 3) the historical lumbering district of Bangor, where the Penobscot River drains into Penobscot Bay.

Each of these three harbors contains a large cluster of light stations. For those wishing to see the greatest amount of lighthouses in the shortest amount of time, the areas of Portland, Bath, and Bangor offer the best opportunities. Let's examine each harbor in a bit more detail:

1) Portland has long been home to the largest seaport in northern New England. Strategic as a shipper and receiver of goods from southern ports such as Boston and New York City. Guiding vessels into Portland's Casco Bay are six light stations:

   - Cape Elizabeth Light
   - Halfway Rock Light
   - Portland Breakwater Light
   - Portland Head Light
   - Ram Island Ledge Light
   - Spring Point Ledge Light

2) Bath is aptly nicknamed "The City of Ships." Since the 1740s, roughly 5,000 vessels have been built and launched from the Bath area, which at one time had more than 200 shipbuilding firms. By the 1850s, Bath became the nation's fifth largest seaport, producing clipper ships that sailed to ports around the world. Because of its strategic positioning and tricky navigation, Bath's Kennebec River and Sagadahoc Bay are home to 11 light stations:

   - Burnt Island Light
   - Cuckolds Light
   - Doubling Point Range Lights
   - Doubling Point Light
   - Hendricks Head Light
   - Pemaquid Point Light

- Perkins Island Light
- Pond Island Light
- Ram Island Light
- Seguin Island Light
- Squirrel Point Light

3) Bangor was once the world's largest lumber port, with 150 sawmills operating along the Penobscot River. In 1850 alone, the city shipped over 150 million board feet of lumber on 3,300 ships which passed by the mills and traveled 30 miles downstream to the mouth of the Atlantic, and from there to ports around the world. Bangor's Penobscot Bay is home to no fewer than 21 light stations:

- Browns Head Light
- Burnt Coat Harbor Light
- Curtis Island Light
- Deer Island Thorofare Light
- Dice Head Light
- Eagle Island Light
- Fort Point Light
- Goose Rocks Light
- Grindle Point Light
- Heron Neck Light
- Indian Island Light
- Isle au Haut Light
- Marshall Point Light
- Owls Head Light
- Pumpkin Island Light
- Rockland Breakwater Harbor Light
- Rockland Harbor Southwest Light
- Saddleback ledge Light
- Tenants Harbor Light
- Two Bush Island Light
- Whitehead Light

Other, lessor, harbors also contain a number of lighthouses. 13 light stations fall into this category including:

- Baker Island Light (Frenchman Bay)
- Bass Harbor Head Light (Bass Harbor)
- Bear Island Light (Northeast Harbor)
- Blue Hill Bay Light (Blue Hill Bay)
- Egg Rock Light (Frenchman Bay)
- Franklin Island Light (Muscongus Bay)
- Lubec Channel Light (Passamaquoddy Bay)
- Narraguagus Light (Pleasant Bay)
- Nash Island Light (Pleasant Bay)
- Prospect Harbor Light (Prospect Harbor)
- Whaleback Light (Portsmouth Harbor)
- Whitlocks Mill Light (Passamaquoddy Bay)
- Winter Harbor Light (Winter Harbor)

The second category of light stations, open water lightouses, includes those that dot the coast, providing a warning to mariners who might wander too close to Maine's rocky shoreline. Widely spaced, these stations were crucial navigational aid in the major shipping lanes linking Maine to Europe and other United States ports. 13 lights fall into this category, including:

- Boon Island Light
- Cape Neddick Light
- Goat Island Light
- Great Duck Island Light
- Libby Island Light
- Little River Light
- Matinicus Rock Light
- Monhegan Island Light
- Moose Peak Light
- Mount Desert Rock Island Light
- Petit Manan Light

- West Quoddy Head Light
- Wood Island Light

Finally, there is one Maine Lighthouse that does not fall into either category:

- Ladies Delight Light

Ladies Delight is the only lighthouse in Maine which does not reside within coastal waters. Instead, this light stands sentry on Lake Cobbosseecontee, in the town of Winthrop. The reason for inclusion of this light is its historical significance - at the time of its construction in 1908, this was the only lighthouse on an inland lake east of the Mississippi. Also noteworthy is its granite construction. Although partly decorative, it has served as a navigational to boaters for over a century.

Resources in this Book

In this book, each of these lighthouses will be scrutinized, using information obtained from the Coast Guard, the National Register of Historic Places, from the current caretakers of these structures, and, finally, from personal observation. Whether you are a casual fan of Maine lighthouses, or a fervent enthusiast, this book should be both enjoyable and informative.

Within these pages, you'll discover how these structures were built with the design details that made each one unique. You'll also discover the best viewing spots for each lighthouse, and the level of accessibility (or inaccessibility) that each one offers. You might even find some anecdotes that have been passed down over generations to help you understand what life was like at these structures during the 1800s. So without further ado, let's begin our journey to Maine's lighthouses!

***

1 Whaleback Light

First Established: 1829
Nearest to: Kittery
Latitude: 43° 03' 31" N
Longitude: 70° 41' 46" W
Tower Height: 70ft
Elevation: 59ft
Design: Conical Tower

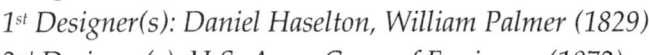
Source: National Archives

1st Designer(s): Daniel Haselton, William Palmer (1829)
2nd Designer(s): U.S. Army Corps of Engineers (1872)
Material: Granite Block
Light Sequence: White light - 0.1 seconds on, 8.4 seconds off, 0.1 seconds on, 1.4 seconds off - repeating
Fog Horn: 2 blasts every 30 seconds

National Register of Historic Places (12/07/1987)

Physical Appearance:

Rising out of a shallow rock outcropping some fifty-nine feet above the mean high water level, the Whaleback Light Station consists of a conical ashlar granite tower abutting a rectangular brick fog signal building. Completed in 1872, this remarkably intact structure houses within its granite walls the former keeper's quarters and storage facilities. It features a vertical row of three windows and a door on its north face. A striking molded granite deck caps the tower shaft and supports an iron walkway with railing. The octagonal lantern is covered by a domed roof surmounted by a spherical ventilator.

Historical Significance:

Established in 1829 and completely rebuilt in 1872, the Whaleback Light Station occupies a shallow rock ledge at the outer entrance to Portsmouth Harbor.

Whaleback light was the second of two lights built to guide vessels along the Piscataqua River. Its location at the outer entrance of the harbor served as a beacon between the Isles of Shoals light off New Hampshire and the inner harbor light that had been established in 1789. During the nineteenth century, Whaleback light was classified as a secondary sea-coast light - an indication of its significance to the proximity of major shipping lanes and the great volume of traffic into and out of the harbors at Portsmouth and Kittery. It was automated in 1963.

Additional Information

Whaleback Light is the Maine's southernmost lighthouse. The lighthouse is located in Kittery at the mouth of the Piscataqua River on a small rock outcropping, approximately 1,500 feet north of the Maine-New Hampshire border.

Because of numerous shipwrecks in the area, in 1827 Congress appropriated a sum of $1,500 in March 1827 for a lighthouse marking the entrance to Portsmouth Harbor. It was quickly learned that this was plainly not enough money to build a rugged lighthouse in such an exposed position. Two more appropriations were made by 1829, for a total of $20,000.

Contractors were hired and work began on the tower foundation. Work on the lower courses could take place only for a few hours around low tide. A lighthouse was eventually erected on a conical granite pier. The 38-foot tower was 22 feet in diameter at its base, and 11 feet at the top.

Over time, it became apparent that the original tower was poorly constructed. A structural examination revealed that the foundation hadn't been leveled before construction began, and that small stones were improperly used to fill in gaps near the bottom of the tower.

After severe storms in 1869 caused more cracks in the tower and foundation, a new lighthouse tower was erected in 1872. The new tower, 27 feet in diameter at its base and about 70 feet tall to the very top of its lantern dome, was constructed of granite blocks dovetailed together in a style that became the norm for lighthouse towers exposed to such harsh conditions.

In 2007, under the provisions of the National Historic Lighthouse Preservation Act of 2000, the American Lighthouse Foundation and its chapter, the Friends of Portsmouth Harbor Lighthouse, applied for the transfer of the lighthouse. In November 2008, the American Lighthouse Foundation was awarded ownership of the lighthouse.

Since then, the lighthouse has been weatherproofed, and the lantern, dome, deck, and other exterior ironwork have been repainted. For more information on restoration progress:
http://www.portsmouthharborlighthouse.org/

Best Viewing

Whaleback Light can be viewed distantly from Fort Foster in Kittery and from Fort Stark and Fort Constitution in Portsmouth, New Hampshire.

For close viewing, it is necessary to travel by boat. Portsmouth Harbor Cruises *http://www.portsmouthharbor.com/* offers a daily 1 ½ hour cruise to Whaleback Light during Spring, Summer, and Fall months.

***

2 Boon Island Light

First Established: 1811
Nearest to: York
Latitude: 43° 07' 14" N
Longitude: 70° 28" 35" W
Tower Height: 133ft
Elevation: 137ft
Design: Conical Tower

Source: National Archives

1st Designer(s): Unknown (1811)
2nd Designer(s): Colonel Seward Merrill (1833)
3rd Designer(s): U.S. Army Corps of Engineers (1855)
Material: Granite Block
Light Sequence: White light – 5 seconds on - repeating
Fog Horn: 1 blast every 10 seconds

National Register of Historic Places (01/28/1988)

Physical Appearance:

At 133 feet in height, the Boon Island Light Tower is the tallest such structure along the Maine coast. The handsome tapered granite tower rises between the ruins of the former keeper's house, and a modern generator shed.

The 1855 tower is constructed of ashlar granite that is punctuated by two opposing vertical rows of seven windows each. A wide conical base supports the shaft of the tower which rises to a wide molded band situated below the protruding parapet.

This narrow parapet frames a tall granite shaft that carries the lantern. A domed roof caps the lantern and its modern beacon. The interior of the tower houses the circular stair that leads to a door at the parapet. Structural reinforcement of the tower was made in 1888 following a severe storm of the previous season. This consisted of the placement of steel bars in the gallery and upper section of the shaft.

Historical Significance:

The Boon Island Light Station towers above this small rock island located approximately six miles off the Maine coast. It contains the tallest light tower in Maine and is the southernmost of the seacoast lights.

Boon Island Light Station was established during the War of 1812, and is the seventh oldest station in Maine. In the 1850s, when a comprehensive classification of lights was instituted, Boon Island was ranked as a primary seacoast station, one of only six such lights in Maine in 1861. Widely spaced along the coast, these stations were crucial navigational aid in the major shipping lanes linking Maine to Europe and other United States ports. In 1978 this station was automated by the Coast Guard, and many of its outbuildings were subsequently removed.

The light tower at Boon Island is the third such structure on the site. The original tower was destroyed in 1831, subsequently rebuilt and then finally replaced by the present granite tower.

Additional Information

Boon Island is the site of the infamous wreck of *Nottingham Galley* in 1710. The ship hit an island outcropping and the crew resorted to cannibalism before eventually being rescued. It is said that ghosts of those who perished still wander the island.

Boon Island light is one of the most isolated lighthouses in Maine, and also one of the most dangerous. The original tower and its replacement tower were both washed away by storms. The third (and current) granite tower survives despite substantial damage received during the blizzard of 1978.

In 2014, the light was sold at auction to a real estate investor for $78,000, who subsequently sold it to a lighthouse enthusiast and philanthropist. Attempts have been made to restore the tower and buildings, but as of this date the island remains inaccessible to the public.

Best Viewing

Boon Island Light can be viewed distantly from Long Beach Road (i.e. Long Sands Beach) and from Sohier Park (where the Nubble Lighthouse is located – see next section), both in York.

For closer viewing, it is necessary to travel by boat. A list of for-hire charter boats is available at:

https://www.maine.gov/dmr/recreational-fishing/forhirefleet/yorkcounty.html

***

3 Cape Neddick Light (The Nubble)

First Established: 1879
Nearest to: York
Latitude: 43° 09' 54" N
Longitude: 70° 35' 27" W
Tower Height: 41ft
Elevation: 88ft

Source: National Archives

Design: Conical Tower
Designer(s): U.S. Army Corps of Engineers (1879)
Material: Cast Iron with Brick Lining
Light Sequence: Red light - 6 seconds on, 6 seconds off - repeating
Fog Horn: 1 blast every 10 seconds

National Register of Historic Places (02/22/1985)

Physical Appearance:

Cape Neddick Light Station, locally known as "The Nubble", is situated on a high piece of land, largely bare rock, off York Beach and is connected by a bar with the mainland at a very low drain of tide.

There are five buildings on the island: the keeper's house, a single gable, one-and-a-half story wood frame structure of six rooms which is connected with the light tower by a covered way; the red brick oil house; the wood frame single-story workshop; and the boat house with ways leading to the water.

The 39 foot light tower is of iron lined with brick and has 32 iron steps leading to the round watch room. Seven more iron steps reach the lantern which has eight panes of glass, four ruby-colored facing the land and the remainder white exposed to the ocean. The tower is equipped with a fourth order light.

Historical Significance:

Cape Neddick Light Station, located on a high promontory reaching out into the Atlantic between Portsmouth and Portland is an important navigational mark guiding sailors away from the jagged rocks at its base. One of the few stations that has never been rebuilt; it has become a mecca for artists and tourists because of its picturesque location and accessibility from the mainland.

Additional Information

Nubble Light is located off Cape Neddick, a village in the town of York. The Nubble got its name due to the fact that it is a thin strip of land with a small island at the tip. It is shaped like the letter "*i*" with the lighthouse being located on the dot of the *i*.

The Nubble Light used a unique cable car system to ferry materials (and sometimes children) between the mainland and the island. This car, which has since been removed, was a wooden box, about five feet square. A cable was suspended on telephone poles that were installed at both ends, and had platforms in place to load and unload whatever was needed. The cables exist to this day and there is talk of restoring the platforms and car.

After being automated in 1987, the light station was leased by the Coast Guard to the town of York in 1989. Under the Maine Lights Program, the lighthouse officially became the property of the town in 1998.

The Nubble Light It is one of the most visited, photographed, and painted lighthouses in Maine. In 1977, it became the only lighthouse in America to go extraterrestrial when NASA sent Voyager II into space carrying a picture of the lighthouse.

In 2018, the keeper's house and light tower were scraped and sandblasted and received a fresh coat of white paint.

Best Viewing

Nubble Island is inaccessible to visitors. However, the light is only a few hundred feet off of Sohier Park in York Beach and can easily be viewed from there. There is a gift shop in the park; proceeds are used for the refurbishment of the buildings.

To visit the Nubble Light, follow Nubble Road in York to Sohier Park. The park contains a large parking lot, gift shop, and restaurant all within clear view of the lighthouse.

***

4 Goat Island Light

First Established: 1833
Nearest to: Cape Porpoise
Latitude: 43° 21' 28" N
Longitude: 70° 25' 30" W
Tower Height: 25ft
Elevation: 38ft
Design: Cylindrical Tower
1st Designer(s): Unknown (1833)
2nd Designer(s): U.S. Army Corps of Engineers (1859)
Material: Brick
Light Sequence: White light – 6 seconds on - repeating
Fog Horn: 1 blast every 15 seconds

Source: National Historic Register

National Register of Historic Places (12/07/1987)

Physical Appearance:

Goat Island Light Station consists of a detached cylindrical brick tower, a one-and-a-half-story frame keeper's house, boathouse and a brick oil house. The dwelling and tower were formerly connected by way of a long covered passageway.

The round configuration of the light tower, built in 1859, clearly indicates its mid-nineteenth century date of construction and thereby its relationship to a number of other Maine lights. The tower is twenty-five feet in height from its base to the center of the octagonal lantern. Its west face is punctuated by a single window near the base. A circular walkway and railing surmount the tower. The lantern is crowned by a spherical ventilator. Jutting from the north of the tower is a small brick workroom containing two doors. It was formerly connected to the long covered passage that extended to the house. An open wooden walkway has replaced this feature.

Facing north, the L-shaped 1859 keeper's house, which is sheathed in clapboards, has a three-bay facade and a pair of gable roofed dormers. A pair of replacement bay windows flank the small, centrally placed gable roofed vestibule. Replacement windows, two on each story, are located in the gable ends. The one-and-a-half-story ell telescopes from the southwest corner. It has a gable roofed dormer on its west side and a one-story wing extending to the south. The rear elevation features a short, enclosed hip roofed porch and a dormer. Documentary photographs of the house show that when it was first built it was covered in board-and-batten siding and had no dormers.

Historical Significance:

The light station at Goat Island was established in 1833 as a guide to the harbor of refuge at Cape Porpoise.

Located on the south side of treeless Goat Island, the light station serves not only as a navigational aid to the entrance of Cape Porpoise Harbor but also as a warning beacon to the numerous small islands and rock shoals that populate this short stretch of coast northeast of Kennebunkport. The original configuration of the station is not positively known, although the 1848 light list indicates that the tower was approximately twenty feet in height. In 1859 the tower and dwelling were pulled down and their present replacements built.

Additional Information

During the presidency of George H. W. Bush, Secret Service agents lived on Goat Island to keep watch while the president visited his home in Kennebunk.

In 1990, Goat Island Light was the final Maine light station to be automated. In 1998, the light station was transferred to the *Kennebunk Conservation Trust*: *http://www.kporttrust.org/kctgoat-island-lighthouse*, who continues to restore the station buildings. Grounds are open to visitors traveling by boat during summer months.

Best Viewing

This lighthouse is located on Goat Island in Cape Porpoise, and can be viewed at a distance from the end of Pier Road in Cape Porpoise.

Goat Island is accessible by boat and is open to the public seasonally. Small boats are allowed to dock during high tide and tour the property. Otherwise, close up viewing can be accomplished via boat cruises originating from area towns. One such cruise is offered by EcoAdventures in Kennebunk: *https://newenglandecoadventures.com/guided-tour-of-goat-island-light-house/*

The Goat Island keeper's house and light tower are open to visitors one day per year on Maine Open Lighthouse Day. More information about this event can be found at:

http://www.lighthousefoundation.org/maine-open-lighthouse-day

***

5 Wood Island Light

First Established: 1808
Nearest to: Biddeford
Latitude: 43° 27' 24" N
Longitude: 70° 19' 44" W
Tower Height: 47ft
Elevation: 71ft
Design: Conical Tower
1st Designer(s): Unknown (1808)
2nd Designer(s): U.S. Army Corp of Engineers (1858)
Material: Granite Block
Light Sequence: Alternating white and green lights – 10 seconds on - repeating
Fog Horn: 2 blasts every 30 seconds

Source: woodislandlighthouse.org

National Register of Historic Places (12/07/1987)

Physical Appearance:

The Wood Island Light Station consists of a conical granite light tower connected via a long narrow passageway to the two-story frame, gambrel roof keeper's house. A stone oil house also survives. Wood Island's light tower, constructed in 1808, stands at a height of forty seven feet from its base to the lens focal plane. Its southeast face is punctuated by a trio of asymmetrically placed window openings which originally contained six-over-six double-hung sash. They illuminate the spiral interior stair. The tower supports an iron walkway with railing and a centrally placed ten-sided lantern.

A small gable roofed frame building with a single window on its east elevation is joined to the southwest face of the tower. Its gable end meets the long, low passageway that extends to the ell of the keeper's house.

Facing south, the keeper's house is sheathed in clapboards and has an enclosed porch across the first story of its facade in addition to a pair of widely spaced gable roofed dormers. Before twentieth century alterations, the porch featured eight coupled posts on brick piers behind which were two windows and a center door. The east gambrel end has a pair of symmetrically placed windows on both stories and three in the ell. The fenestration pattern in the main block is repeated on the west end. At the rear a shed addition with one window abuts the junction of the front block and ell. The ell contains a second story window and a pent gable end. A pair of brick flues punctuates the roof ridge of the main building and the ell respectively.

Historical Significance:

Wood Island Light Station was one of two lights established in 1808; the other being at West Quoddy Head in eastern Maine.

Wood Island light was erected on a small shallow island located at the mouth of the Saco River. This location was of particular significance due to the heavy maritime traffic in and around the commercial centers of Saco and Biddeford. Both of these communities had developed into important local trading centers during the eighteenth century, and their growth continued into the 1800s. Until the construction of Whaleback light in 1829, the station at Wood Island was the southernmost of the principle aids to navigation in Maine.

Additional Information

This lighthouse is located on Wood Island just east of the mouth of the Saco River, near the Biddeford Pool area.

In 1808, a 45-foot octagonal wooden lighthouse was constructed and went into service the following year. This tower operated until 1839, when a new 44-foot conical rubblestone tower—20 feet in diameter at the base and 10 feet at the top—was built, along with a new one-story granite dwelling. The revolving light was 69 feet above mean high water.

In early 2003, a chapter of the American Lighthouse Foundation was formed to care for the light station. The group, Friends of Wood Island Lighthouse, has been working for a full restoration of the lighthouse tower, keeper's house, boathouse, and oil house. The group also takes care of the wooden boardwalk from the boathouse to the keeper's house and seven acres of land at the light station.

In the fall of 2009, work began on the restoration of the lighthouse tower. The work was completed in the summer of 2010.

The light is open to the public through The Friends of Wood Island Lighthouse:
http://www.woodislandlighthouse.org

Approximately 30 acres of Wood Island is also protected by the Audubon Society as a bird sanctuary that provides an area for nesting as well as an important stop for migration.

Best Viewing

Wood Island Light can be seen from a distance from the Biddeford Pool. Scheduled tours are available through The Friends of Wood Island Lighthouse. Visitors meet their tour host at Vines Landing 30 minutes before the boat departs and take a short 15 minute boat ride across Winter Harbor to the Wood Island boat ramp.

This tour includes narration from a tour host and an optional climb up the 60 steps to the top of the light tower.

The Wood Island keeper's house and light tower are open to visitors one day per year on Maine Open Lighthouse Day. More information about this event can be found at:

http://www.lighthousefoundation.org/maine-open-lighthouse-day

6 Cape Elizabeth Light (Two Lights)

First Established: 1828
Nearest to: Cape Elizabeth
Latitude: 43° 33' 57" N
Longitude: 70° 12' 00" W
Tower Height: 65ft
Elevation: 129ft

Source: National Archives

Design: Conical Tower
1st Designer: Jeremiah Berry (1828)
2nd Designer: U.S. Army Corps of Engineers (1874)
Material: Cast Iron
Light Sequence: White light - 0.3 seconds on, 2.2 seconds off, 0.3 seconds on, 2.2 seconds off, 0.3 seconds on, 2.2seconds off, 0.3 seconds on, 7.2 seconds off - repeating
Fog Horn: 2 blasts every 60 seconds

National Register of Historic Places (11/11/1974)

Physical Appearance:

The two cast iron lighthouses on the Cape Elizabeth shore were erected a century ago in 1874. Located 300 yards apart, they were of identical design. Both lights stand 129 feet above sea level and are 65 feet high. While the west light became altered into an observation post during World War II, the east light retains the original appearance which both once had.

The main shaft of the lighthouse is comprised of six stages, each one divided by a projecting circular ridge at the top and bottom. The stages decrease slightly in size as the shaft rises. The first, third, and fifth stages each contain a window on the east and west sides of the light. This Italianate architectural detail is fashioned out of cast iron. Another handsome cast iron element is the circular balcony located at the sixth stage. Supported by a series of brackets, the balcony has a railing which features delicately turned posts.

The top of the lighthouse contains the beacon, originally kerosene but electric since 1925. The beacon is surrounded by glass and has a domed roof which is capped by a large ball. A second, less ornamental cast iron balcony encircles the base of the beacon area. The two balconies are joined by a cast iron ladder.

Cape Elizabeth's "Two Lights", as they are popularly known, stand as a graphic reminder of an era a century ago in which even the most functional of structures were endowed with a proud grace and dignity of design.

Historical Significance:

The location of this lighted beacon is one of the most important along the northeast coast of the United States. Not only does it mark the entrance to Portland Harbor but it is also a key landmark in coastal navigation. These twin towers also represent an era when the use of double lights for ranging purposes was adopted in several locations.

As early as 1811, a 50 ft. rubblestone and lime mortar tower was erected on the site of the present east light by Gen. Henry Dearborn of Revolutionary War fame. In the second decade of the 19th century a rapid growth in shipping occurred and in the spring of 1827, the Federal Government approved the erection of twin 65 ft. stone beacons 129 ft. above sea level. Located 300 yards apart, the eastern tower showed a fixed light and the western a flashing light 45 seconds on and 45 off. In 1854, the new Fresnel lenses were added to both lights.

Suddenly on June 1, 1855, it was announced that the western light would be discontinued and on August 1, it was extinguished. Such a storm of protest followed, particularly on the part of fishermen who used the lights for triangulating the position of nets and traps, that on April 1, 1856 both lights were restored to their former state. It was not the last such episode.

The Lighthouse Board, in an economy move in 1882 again eliminated the western light, and again there was a great public outcry. Through the influence of Maine's powerful congressman, Thomas B. Reed, this ruling was overturned.

Finally, despite more protests, the western light was permanently extinguished in 1924. During the Second World War, it was stripped of its lantern and used as an observation post. In 1959, the west tower along with 10.5 acres was sold to the highest bidder.

Additional Information

The Cape Elizabeth lights are unique in that they were designed as "ranging" lights, sometimes also called "leading" lights. The lights were considered among the most important on the Maine coast. The reason for the east-west orientation of the lights was so mariners approaching Portland Harbor could line them up to know they were safely on course.

In 1872, the Lighthouse Board announced that the two rubblestone towers built in 1828 had deteriorated to the point that they had to be rebuilt. A pair of identical 67-foot cast-iron towers replaced the original towers in 1874. The cast-iron segments of these towers were very similar to those used in the building of the Cape Neddick lighthouse in 1879.

The east lighthouse was the subject of a famous Edward Hopper 1929 painting "The Lighthouse of Two Lights." In 1970, Hopper's painting became the basis of the first lighthouse to appear on a U.S. postage stamp, commemorating Maine's sesquicentennial.

Best Viewing

A mainland lighthouse, Cape Elizabeth Light is located in Cape Elizabeth at Two Lights State Park, located off Route 77. The lighthouse and grounds are privately owned and not open to the public but can be viewed from the park at the end of Two Lights Road. For those a bit more adventurous, a short walk up Two Lights Terrace and Beacon Lane provide a closer look.

7 Portland Head Light

First Established: 1790
Nearest to: Cape Elizabeth
Latitude: 43° 37' 23" N
Longitude: 70° 12' 28" W
Tower Height: 80ft
Elevation: 102ft
Design: Conical Tower

Source: National Historic Register

Designer(s): John Nichols, Jonathan Bryant
Material: Rubblestone/Brick
Light Sequence: White light – 4 seconds on - repeating
Fog Horn: 1 blast every 15 seconds

National Register of Historic Places (02/15/1973)

Physical Appearance:

Portland Headlight, completed in 1790, is located at Portland Head in the town of Cape Elizabeth. It sets high on a rocky promontory jutting into the sea at Casco Bay.

Within the complex of buildings at the site are the light tower, keepers' quarters, whistle house, paint locker and garage. The tower is constructed of random stone rubble from the base to a stone ledge. There is a brick course from the ledge to the metal light housing.

The tower room and whistle house are also constructed of stone and brick. The keepers' quarters is a wood frame building finished in clapboards and shingles. All of the buildings are set upon stone and brick masonry foundations.

The keepers' quarters is a two-and-a-half story duplex with a combination of gable and hip roof construction. There is a living room, dining room and kitchen on each side of the first floor. There are three bedrooms and both on each side of the second floor.

Historical Significance:

Portland Headlight is one of the four lighthouses in existence whose construction was authorized by President Washington, and that has never been rebuilt. The main section of the tower remains today in the same form as when it was completed in 1790. It was first lighted on January 10, 1791. The tower was constructed of rubblestone taken from nearby fields and the shore. The builders were John Nichols and Jonathan Bryant, two local masons. Bryant also had his own lime kiln where he burned limestone from the quarries in Rockland.

The original structure was 72' high with a 15' lantern. In 1813, twenty feet was removed from the tower and in 1883 another 21 feet was removed. Due to public reaction, it was raised again with brickwork in 1885. In 1900, it was repaired using the original stones from the section that had been removed in 1813.

The first keepers' quarters was built in 1816 and was a 34' x 20' one story cottage. The present keepers' quarters was built in 1891 upon the foundation of the old cottage.

Portland Headlight has been and remains as an important part of the Maine scene and as an important part of her history. She has stood for nearly two centuries as a beacon for the commerce of the United States and other nations. She is perhaps the most well known and most photographed lighthouse on the northeast coast, as well as being a significant part of Maine's history.

Additional Information

Despite the fact that Portland was America's sixth busiest port in the late 1700s, there were no lighthouses within Portland Harbor, or anywhere else along the coast of Maine for that matter.

Concerned with the impact shipwrecks were having on their businesses, 74 Portland merchants petitioned the Massachusetts government in 1784 for a light to be placed at Portland Head to mark the entrance to Portland Harbor. $700 was appropriated and construction began in 1787, but work was soon halted due to lack of funds.

In 1789, mere months into the presidency of George Washington, Congress appropriated an additional $1,500 to be used to complete construction of the light tower. Portland Head Light was therefore the first lighthouse to be paid for by the newly formed federal government.

The rubblestone lighthouse was built by local masons. The original plan called for a 58-foot tower, but during construction it was apparent that the light would be blocked from the south so it was decided to raise tower to 72 feet in height. After the original construction was completed, the light tower received numerous upgrades and downgrades over the next 100 years.

By 1810, the light tower and keeper's house were in poor condition - the woodwork was damp and rotting. Historical documents indicate that repairs were made, but specific references to the repairs are not known.

In 1812, the tower continued to have problems with leaks. A report from that year indicated that the upper portion of the tower was poorly built. The lantern, which was only 5 feet in diameter, was felt to be insufficient. Based on this report, 25 feet of stone was removed from the tower top, and a new lantern was installed.

Improvements continued in subsequent years. In 1855, a fourth-order Fresnel lens replaced the locally-made lamp, the tower was lined with brick, and a cast-iron spiral stairway was built.

In 1864 the light was further improved as an upgraded second-order Fresnel lens was installed. The tower was raised 20 feet, bringing it back to near its original height.

With the completion of Halfway Rock Light in 1871, the Lighthouse Board felt that Portland Head Light had become less important. The tower was again shortened by 20 feet in 1883 and the second-order lens reverted back to a weaker fourth-order lens. Apparently, this did not sit well with mariners, so, a year later, the tower was restored to its former height and a second-order lens was again installed, lighted on January 15, 1885.

Portland Head Light was electrified in 1929. As with many other lights on the eastern seaboard, the light tower went dark for three years during World War II. In 1958, the second-order Fresnel lens was removed and replaced by aerobeacons.

On August 7, 1989, a celebration commemorating the 200th anniversary of the Lighthouse Service was held at Portland Head Light. That same day, the light was automated and the Coast Guard keepers were reassigned.

A museum was opened in the former keeper's house in 1992. Among the displays are the tower's original second order Fresnel lens. In October 1993, the light station was deeded to the Town of Cape Elizabeth.

Best Viewing

The Portland Head Light is located within Fort Williams Park on 1000 Shore Road in Cape Elizabeth.

This mainland lighthouse is accessible to the public and can be accessed by visiting Fort Williams.

The light tower at Portland Head Light is open to visitors (on a limited basis) one day per year on Maine Open Lighthouse Day. More information about this event can be found at:

http://www.lighthousefoundation.org/maine-open-lighthouse-day/

***

8 Ram Island Ledge Light

First Established: 1905
Nearest to: Cape Elizabeth
Latitude: 43° 37' 53" N
Longitude: 70° 11' 14" W
Tower Height: 77ft
Elevation: 78ft

Source: U.S. Coast Guard

Design: Conical Tower
Designer(s): U.S. Army Corps of Engineers (1905)
Material: Granite Block
Light Sequence: White light – 6 seconds on - repeating
Fog Horn: 1 blast every 10 seconds

National Register of Historic Places (01/29/1988)

Physical Appearance:

Standing on a rock outcropping that is barely visible at high tide, the Ram Island Ledge Light Station, built in 1905, consists of a conical granite tower and an attached skeleton pier. The keeper's quarters and storage facilities are located within the tower wall. This tower rises to a height of seventy-seven feet from its base to the middle of the round lantern. A door reached by a ladder rising from the pier is located in the west face below a small square window. A pair of windows punctuate the south side and one is located in the east face. A wide molded granite walkway caps the tower base. It is framed by an iron railing. The unusual round lantern features an iron base and diamond pane windows sheltering the modern beacon.

Historical Significance:

Ram Island Ledge Light Station was established in 1905 to mark the hazardous and oftentimes submerged shoals that populate the northern side of the entrance to Portland Harbor.

In 1902, Congress appropriated $83,000 toward a projected estimate of $166,000 for the construction of a light station on Ram Island Ledge. This action was taken after the steamship *California* ran aground on the ledge in 1900. Work had not begun, however, before the British schooner *Glenrosa* struck the reef during a heavy fog on September 22, 1902. She was followed to her demise less than three months later by the fishing schooner *Cora* and *Lillian*. These three mishaps clearly illustrated the need for a light and fog signal at this location in the busy shipping lanes near Portland. The light was exhibited for the first time on April 10, 1905. Sixty years later it was automated.

Additional Information

Ram Island Ledge Light has a granite tower that is nearly identical to Graves Light in Boston, which was built one year after the Ram Island Ledge Light was completed.

Building a lighthouse on a mostly submerged rock outcropping was no easy task. A total of 669 four-ton granite blocks were quarried in Vinalhaven and assembled at the ledge.

Ram Island Ledge Light is unique as one of Maine's few lighthouses where the keeper's quarters were located inside the light tower. Before the light was automated, keepers stayed for two weeks, with daily 12-hour shifts, followed by a week of shore leave.

Offers by the Coast Guard to transfer the light to non-profit organizations failed in 1998 and again in 2009. So, in 2010, Ram Island Ledge Light was put up for public bid in an online auction. The winning bid of $190,000 was made by a Maine neurosurgeon who said he simply wanted to preserve this historic site.

Best Viewing

Ram Island Ledge Light is located at the northern approach to Portland Harbor in Casco Bay, nearest to the town of Cape Elizabeth. This light is not accessible to the public, but can be viewed distantly from Fort Williams Park, home of the Portland Head Light, or by boat tour.

Portland Discovery Land and Sea Tours offers a 60-minute "Lighthouse Lovers" boat tour which cruises past Ram Island Ledge Light and several other lights in Portland Harbor during summer months. For more information visit:

http://www.portlanddiscovery.com/tours/lighthouse-lovers-cruise

***

9 Spring Point Ledge Light

First Established: 1897
Nearest to: South Portland
Latitude: 43° 39' 07" N
Longitude: 70° 13' 26" W
Tower Height: 25ft
Elevation: 54ft
Design: Spark Plug
Designer(s): U.S. Army Corps of Engineers (1897)
Material: Cast Iron/Brick
Light Sequence: Red or white light, depending on heading – 6 seconds on - repeating
Fog Horn: 1 blast every 10 seconds

Source: National Historic Register

National Register of Historic Places (12/07/1987)

Physical Appearance:

The Spring Point Ledge Light Station is one of four similarly shaped "spark plug" structures built in Maine during the 1890s, three of which survive. This particular example is unique among the group because it retains the gallery that encircles the top of the base. It was erected in 1896-97.

This handsome structure consists of a poured concrete base encased in cast iron plates. The gallery is supported by large iron brackets with pendants and is sheltered by a shallow roof. A railing extends around the walkway. The broad second stage of the tower contains the four-level keeper's quarters and storage facilities. Its cast iron structure is punctuated by a number of window openings (all containing glass blocks) and a single door. A parapet with railing crowns the second stage, and it is partially supported by iron brackets. The much narrower third stage supports the ten sided iron lantern and its encircling walkway. In 1952 a granite breakwater, 900 feet in length, was completed thereby connecting the light with the mainland.

Historical Significance:

Established in 1897 above a dangerous reef in Portland's inner harbor, the Spring Point Ledge Light Station is the most intact of Maine's three surviving "spark plug" lights.

Spring Point Ledge light is one of two lights that aid navigation in Portland Harbor. The other, Portland Breakwater, was established in 1855. Throughout the latter half of the nineteenth century there was considerable local clamor for a permanent light to mark this particular section of Portland's busy harbor area. The ledge was witness to a number of wrecks and accidental groundings. After repeated requests in the Annual Report(s) of the Light-House Board beginning in 1892, Congress authorized construction of a light station at this site in 1895.

Additional Information

Spring Point Ledge Light is similar in construction to the 2 other existing spark plug lighthouses in Maine:

- 40 Goose Rocks Light
- 62 Lubec Channel Light

As with those lights, a cast iron caisson was constructed, sunken, and filled with concrete. Unlike the other two spark plug lights, however, the Spring Point Light tower built onto the caisson was of brick construction, instead of also being constructed of cast iron.

In 1951, a 900 foot breakwater was added, consisting of 50,000 tons of granite, making Spring Point Ledge Light the first and only caisson-style light station in the United States that visitors can walk to.

The light was automated in 1960. Under the Maine Lights Program, the City of South Portland applied to co-own the property with Southern Maine Technical College, but in October 1997 the city council voted to withdraw the application after a handicapped-rights activist had threatened to take the city to court if the lighthouse wasn't made handicapped-accessible.

In March 1998, the Spring Point Museum (now the Portland Harbor Museum) also applied to the Maine Lights Selection Committee. The museum formed the *Spring Point Ledge Light Trust*, and the museum answered the handicapped access issue by pointing out that the Army Corps of Engineers owns the breakwater, therefore the owner of the lighthouse is not legally responsible for access.

On April 28, 1998, the Maine Lights Selection Committee announced the transfer of Spring Point Ledge Light to the Trust: *http://springpointlight.org/*

Since then, many improvements to the light have been made, including replacing the badly deteriorated iron canopy over the structure's lower gallery. The group has stated its future plans include restoration of the submerged caisson.

Best Viewing

Spring Point Ledge Light is located at the western approach to Portland Harbor, nearest to the city of South Portland. It is accessible to the public and can be viewed by walking to the end of the breakwater that it is located on Fort Road in South Portland, on the campus of Southern Maine Community College.

Periodic tours of the light are available through the Spring Point Light Trust (use the link above for info.)

According to the website: *"Our all-volunteer staff open[s] the lighthouse for tours when possible, most Tuesdays and some Saturdays and Sundays between Memorial Day Weekend and Labor Day Weekend."*

Spring Point Ledge Light is also open to visitors one day per year on Maine Open Lighthouse Day. More information about this event can be found at:

http://www.lighthousefoundation.org/maine-open-lighthouse-day

10 Portland Breakwater Light (Bug Light)

First Established: 1855
Nearest to: South Portland
Latitude: 43° 39' 19" N
Longitude: 70° 14' 05" W
Tower Height: 26ft
Elevation: 39ft
Design: Greek Revival Tower

Source: National Historic Register

1st Designer(s): Unknown (1855)
2nd Designer(s): Thomas Ustick Walter (1875 – unverified)
Material: Cast Iron/Brick
Light Sequence: White light – flashing every 4 seconds
Fog Horn: No fog signal

National Register of Historic Places (01/23/1973)

Physical Appearance:

This structure is unique because of its construction and decoration. It is possible that Thomas Ustick Walter, who designed and erected the National Capitol's cast iron dome, might have had something to do with the structure; especially since its details, derived from the fourth-century B.C. Choragic Monument of Lysikrates in Athens, show an archeological bias consistent with Walter's academic tastes.

Erected in 1855, the structure is a circular tower 11'-8" in diameter of cast-iron plates fashioned as fluted columns with Corinthian capitals covering joints. The lighthouse is situated on a stone base at the end of the breakwater. The walls are 6" thick composed of 1" cast-iron plates bolted at the flanges. The remainder of the 6" thickness consists of 4" of brick filler, plastered inside. There is an airspace between the iron plate and brick. Cast-iron columns cover the bolted flanges of the plates.

Historical Significance:

This Greek Revival structure was first built in 1855 and rebuilt in 1875. The structure was abandoned in 1943. The rebuilding in 1875 did not alter the design or character of the structure.

The significance of Portland Breakwater Light is its unique style and construction as shown in the photographs. It also represents the sea-going heritage of the State of Maine in the 18th and 19th centuries when it and its sister lighthouses along Maine's rocky coasts stood as symbols of commercial prosperity derived from shipping.

Built to communicate the location of Portland Breakwater to ships at sea, it also indicates the concern of 19th century Americans to make as essentially functional structure aesthetically pleasing to the eye. Its Greek Revival style would have integrated well into the panorama of Portland in 1855.

Additional Information

The light was nicknamed "Bug Light" due to its small size. The original 1855 structure was an octagonal wooden tower which was removed and replaced by the current cast iron structure in 1875.

The design of this 24-foot-tall, cast-iron tower is unique. The cylinder, a little less than 12 feet in diameter, is surrounded by six fluted columns. It is not clear why such an ornate design was chosen for this light, but it has been suggested that Thomas Ustick Walter, who designed the cast-iron dome on the U.S. Capitol building, may have been involved in designing the Greek-revival ornamentation on the lighthouse.

A keeper's quarters, attached to the western end of the tower, was built in 1889, but demolished in 1934.

The light was deemed unnecessary by the Coast Guard and discontinued June 1942. In 1973, the *South Portland Rotary Club* and *Spring Point Ledge Light Trust* refurbished the lighthouse, and it was relighted as a private aid to navigation in a ceremony on August 14, 2002.

Best Viewing

This lighthouse is located in Bug Light Park in South Portland. Bug Light can be accessed by visiting Bug Light Park on Madison Street. The lighthouse is also visible from the Eastern Promenade in Portland. The grounds are open to the public, but the light tower is not.

However, the light tower is open to visitors one day per year on Maine Open Lighthouse Day. More information about this event can be found at:

http://www.lighthousefoundation.org/maine-open-lighthouse-day

***

11 Halfway Rock Light

Year Established: 1871
Nearest to: Phippsburg
Latitude: 43° 39' 20" N
Longitude: 70° 02' 12" W
Tower Height: 76ft
Elevation: 77ft
Design: Conical Tower
Designer(s): U.S. Army Corps of Engineers
Material: Granite Block
Light Sequence: Red light – 5 seconds on - repeating
Fog Horn: 2 blasts every 30 seconds

Source: National Archives

National Register of Historic Places (01/02/1983)

Physical Appearance:

Standing on a rock outcropping in Casco Bay, the Halfway Rock Light Station, built in 1871, is composed of a tall tapered granite tower connected to a boathouse.

The Halfway Rock light tower rises to a height of nearly sixty-six feet from its base to the middle of its prominent lantern. Its quarry faced granite shaft is punctuated by a vertical row of four windows on both the north and south faces, and a single window in the west side. The base is crowned by a molded granite cornice that is capped by a steel deck and railing. The interior stair leads into the cast iron base that supports the lantern. A door opens off of this base onto the deck surmounting the tower. From here a ladder rises to the narrow walkway which enframes the twelve-sided lantern and its dome shaped iron roof. The tower contains within its walls the keeper's house and storage facilities.

Projecting from the north face of the tower the boathouse is a rectangular brick building. Small windows punctuate each side elevation and a door, formerly sheltered by a narrow shed roofed vestibule, is positioned on the west elevation. A boat slip extends from the gable end of the building.

Historical Significance:

Halfway Rock Light Station, which occupies a shallow rock ledge in Casco Bay, was established in 1871 to mark this dangerous position in a very heavily trafficked approach to Portland.

The 1867 Report of the Light-House Board states that *"...an estimate of appropriation required to mark with a lighthouse this dangerous rock was submitted to Congress at its last session...."* It was not until 1869, however, that construction of the light was authorized and an appropriation of $50,000 made for it. The station was made operational in August 15, 1871, by which time the boathouse and slip were completed. In 1888 a pyramidal skeleton bell tower was added to the site; in 1889 a new boathouse was built. An oil house was constructed on a pyramidal skeleton frame in 1890; and a fog signal was established prior to 1905. The light was automated in 1975.

Additional Information

Halfway Rock is a remote windswept rocky ledge, roughly nine miles east of Portland Head. Construction in this harsh location proved difficult, but the tower's dovetailed granite blocks have stood the test of time. This type of construction is indicative of Maine's offshore light towers, and may have been influenced by the prior work on other light towers performed by Alexander Parris.

The light was automated by the Coast Guard in 1975. By the 2000s, Halfway Rock Light was expected to be transferred to a local nonprofit group or community under the Maine Lights Program, but there were no applicants.

In 2012, the Coast Guard announced that the lighthouse was again available to non-profits under the Historic Lighthouse Preservation Act, but, again there was no interest.

Consequently, the island and light structure were auctioned in 2014 and sold to a Cumberland man who felt "It would be tragic not to restore it."

The new owner soon began rebuilding the boat landing ramp, the attached two-story keeper's building, and the light tower. The restoration work is documented in the book *"Halfway Rock Light Station"* which is currently available for purchase: *http://halfwayrock.com/*

Best Viewing

Halfway Rock Light is located in Casco Bay, roughly halfway between Cape Elizabeth and Cape Small in Phippsburg, giving the light its name.

The light is privately owned and inaccessible to the public. It can be distantly seen from Portland Observatory on Munjoy Hill in Portland and from Lands End on Bailey Island.

Casco Bay Adventures offers lighthouse cruises from Peaks Island, including a ½ day cruise to Halfway Rock Light: *http://www.cascobayadventures.com/*

***

12 Seguin Island Light

Year Established: 1796
Nearest to: Georgetown
Latitude: 43° 42' 26" N
Longitude: 69° 45' 28" W
Tower Height: 53ft
Elevation: 180ft
Design: Conical Tower
1st Designer(s): Henry Dearborn (1796)
2nd Designer(s): Unknown (1820)
3rd Designer(s): U.S. Army Corps of Engineers (1855)
Material: Granite Block
Light Sequence: White light - continuous
Fog Horn: 2 blasts every 20 seconds

Source: seguinisland.org

National Register of Historic Places (05/03/1976)

Physical Appearance:

Seguin Island Light Station occupies the entire Seguin Island in, Georgetown, Maine. One half of the island was ceded to the Federal Government by the Commonwealth of Massachusetts in 1794, the remainder in 1797. All of the improvements on the island have been constructed by the U.S. Coast Guard or its predecessors.

Historical Significance:

Seguin Island Light Station is the second oldest on the Coast of Maine, with construction having started in 1790, five years after the completion of Portland Head Light. The original wooden tower was completed in 1797 at a cost of $6,300. This was replaced in 1820 by a stone tower costing $2,500. In 1857, the present granite structure was erected at a cost of $35,000. Replacement of the first two towers was probably necessitated, or at least hastened, by the damp climate of Seguin Island, which has experienced as many as 2,734 hours of fog in one year (31% of all hours), making it the foggiest light station in the U.S.

The tower is only 53 feet high. However, because of the headland which the tower stands upon, the focal plane of the light is 180 feet above the sea.

Additional Information

There are several theories as to the origin of the word Seguin. One explanation is that the island resembles a tortoise, which Native Americans referred to as "Siguenoc." Another view is that the name is derived from the Algonquin word "Segunau," meaning "alone out to sea." Yet another claim is that Seguin is a poor English translation of a Native American word meaning "place where the sea vomits." Finally, the simplest explanation is that of the Abnaki, where "Sigan" simply means hump.

No matter where the name originated, Seguin Island Light, Maine's 2nd light station, went into service in 1795 with a wooden 33 foot octagonal tower and a one-story dwelling at the summit of Seguin Island, two miles south of the mouth of the Kennebec River in Sagadahoc Bay. The wooden tower was replaced in 1819 with a 20 foot conical granite tower, but due to deteriorating conditions, a new 53 foot whitewashed stone tower with brick one-and-one-half story duplex dwelling were completed in 1853.

The light tower was fitted with the most powerful beacon in Maine – a 12 foot, first- order Fresnel Lens. Automated in 1985, the highest lighthouse in Maine continues to show its fixed white light 180 feet above the Atlantic with at a focal plane of 18 nautical miles.

In 1998, the 10 acre lighthouse and property was transferred to the *Friends of Seguin Light Station* (FOSILS): https://www.seguinisland.org/

FOSILS restored the dwelling and successfully petitioned Congress to prevent the Coast Guard from replacing the historic 1st order Fresnel lens with a modern optic.

Best Viewing

This light is located near Popham Beach ½ mile south of the Kennebec River, nearest to the town of Georgetown.

Grounds are open to the public in season. Hosts give guided tours of the lighthouse and attached museum Memorial Day through Labor Day. Overnight stays are available to FOSIL members.

The lighthouse can be viewed at a distance from Popham Beach, but is best viewed by traveling by boat to the island. Several public boat tours are available, including one from the Maine Maritime Museum in Bath: https://www.mainemaritimemuseum.org/

And via the Seguin Island Ferry in Popham Beach: http://www.fishntripsmaine.com/seguinislandferry.html

Seguin Island Light is open to visitors one day per year on Maine Open Lighthouse Day. More information about this event can be found at:

http://www.lighthousefoundation.org/maine-open-lighthouse-day

***

13 Pond Island Light

Year Established: 1821
Nearest to: Georgetown
Latitude: 43° 44' 24" N
Longitude: 69° 46' 13" W
Tower Height: 20ft
Elevation: 52ft
Design: Cylindrical Tower
1st Designer(s): Unknown (1821)
2nd Designer(s): Unknown (1835)
3rd Designer(s): Unknown (1855)
Material: Brick
Light Sequence: White light - 6 seconds on, 6 seconds off - repeating
Fog Horn: 2 blasts every 30 seconds

Source: U.S. Coast Guard

Lighthouse Appearance and History

Pond Island Light is one of only ten Maine lighthouses which are not registered with the National Register of Historic Places.

Interestingly, no pond exists on 10-acre Pond Island, located on the western mouth of the Kennebec River. The reason for the naming of this island has been lost to history.

Pond Island's 1821 lighthouse was a 12 foot conical stone tower. The tower was accompanied by a stone dwelling for the keeper, with three rooms on the first floor and two small chambers in the attic. Unfortunately, these structures were poorly built and lasted little more than a decade.

In March of 1835, the district lighthouse superintendent advertised for proposals to build a new stone tower, 13 feet tall to the base of the lantern, 14 feet in diameter at the base and 10 feet at the top. The tower was to be topped by a 7-foot octagonal iron lantern, with a fixed white light 55 feet above mean high water.

The 2nd structure, constructed using slate mined from the island, also began to deteriorate until 1855, when the 3rd and current 16½ foot cylindrical white brick tower was built, along with a 1½ story wooden keeper's house.

The light was automated by the Coast Guard in 1960, and in 1962 all buildings except the tower were regrettably demolished. Under the Maine Lights Program, the lighthouse became the property of the U.S. Fish and Wildlife Service in 1998. According to their website:

"Once essential for safe maritime travel, lighthouses now provide sanctuary for nesting seabirds. Eight lighthouse islands on the Maine coast have been transferred from the U.S. Coast Guard to the refuge."

https://www.fws.gov/refuge/Maine_Coastal_Islands/about/lighthouses.html

Best Viewing

Pond Island Light is located near Popham Beach south of the Kennebec River mouth, nearest to the town on Georgetown.

As with many lighthouses in Sagadahoc Bay, Pond Island Light is best viewed by boat. Several public boat tours are available, including one from the Maine Maritime Museum in Bath:
https://www.mainemaritimemuseum.org/

14 Perkins Island Light

Year Established: 1898
Nearest to: Georgetown
Latitude: 43° 47' 12" N
Longitude: 69° 47' 06" W
Tower Height: 17ft
Elevation: 41ft

Source: National Archives

Design: Octagonal Tower
Designer(s): U.S. Army Corps of Engineers (1898)
Material: Shingled Wood Frame
Light Sequence: Red or white light, depending on heading – 2.5 seconds on - repeating
Fog Horn: No fog signal

National Register of Historic Places (12/07/1987)

Physical Appearance:

Situated along the east bank of the Kennebec River, the Perkins Island Light Station is composed of a tapered octagonal frame light tower, a two-story L-shaped keeper's house, a pyramidal bell tower, a brick oil house, and a detached barn. The buildings stand on a rock ledge.

Like the tower erected upriver at Squirrel Point Light Station, the Perkins Island light, which was built in 1898, is a short (seventeen feet from base to center of the lantern) frame structure sheathed in wood shingles. It rests on a stone foundation. A door located on the east elevation opens into the tower and the interior stair. This leads to a wooden exterior gallery added in 1899 that is supported by brackets and located below the lantern. The eight large red panes of glass in the lantern are capped by an octagonal roof surmounted by a spherical ventilator.

Standing to the south of the tower is the keeper's dwelling, also constructed in 1898. Covered in wood shingles, the house's two-story ell faces the river. It extends from the southwest corner of the main block and is flanked by a screened hip roofed porch on the north side and a one-room hip roofed shed with an engaged porch on the south elevation. There are three window openings (all boarded shut) in the ell's west gable and, a window in the south end of the main block and a trio of windows in the north gable end. Additional openings are located on the east elevation. A brick flue rises through the roof at the intersection of the ridges.

Historical Significance:

Occupying a bold rock ledge on the west side of Perkins Island, the Perkins Island Light Station is the southernmost of the four stations erected in 1898 along the Kennebec River.

The Perkins Island Light Station, like its sister lights, was built in response to the need for Federally operated and maintained aids to navigation along this important commercial waterway. In its Annual Report of 1892, the Lighthouse Board described the nature and amount of traffic on the Kennebec and requested funding for the construction of four stations. Congressional action was delayed on the request until 1895 when $17,000 was appropriated for the undertaking. In 1898 the system was completed and placed in operation. The station was automated in 1959 and the buildings transferred to the State of Maine in the 1960s.

Additional Information

Perkins Island Light was the southernmost of four lighthouses constructed during the 1890s to aid vessels traveling up the Kennebec River from Popham Beach to Bath, after passing the earlier light stations established in Sagadahoc Bay at Seguin and Pond Islands.

This light is located on Perkins Island in the Kennebec River, closest to the town of Georgetown.

The light was automated in 1959 by the Coast Guard. All the buildings except the lighthouse tower were demolished and the island was transferred to the State of Maine in the 1960s. In late 2000, a restoration of the bell tower took place, funded by the *Maine Department of Conservation*, and administered by the *Maine Historic Preservation Commission*.

Although the light tower itself is sturdy and the bell tower had been restored, the keeper's house fell into a state of severe disrepair. As a result, an effort began in 2014 by a chapter of the *American Lighthouse Federation*, the *Friends of Perkins Island Lighthouse*, to fully restore the keeper's structure. To date, the exterior has been fully restored and plans are being made for further work. More information about this refurbishment project can be found in the links below:

http://www.lighthousefoundation.org/2014/04/facelift-planned-for-perkins-island-keepers-house/

http://www.lighthousefoundation.org/2015/01/celebrating-perkins-island-light-station/

Best Viewing

Perkins Island and its structures are closed to the public. A distant view can be made from Parker Head Road in Phippsburg, but the light is best viewed by boat cruises along the Kennebec River. Several popular lighthouse cruises are hosted by the Maine Maritime Museum in Bath: *https://www.mainemaritimemuseum.org/*

According to the Museum website:

Midcoast Lights and Rivers (3 hours)

"On this cruise you'll see six lighthouses: Doubling Point Light, the Kennebec Range Lights, Squirrel Point Light, **Perkins Island Light***, Pond Island Light, and Seguin Island Light. Travel the winding Sasanoa River, and weather permitting, cruise the Sheepscot River past Hendricks Head Lighthouse."*

15 Squirrel Point Light

Year Established: 1898
Nearest to: Arrowsic
Latitude: 43° 48' 59" N
Longitude: 69° 48' 08" W
Tower Height: 25ft
Elevation: 33ft
Design: Octagonal Tower
Designer(s): U.S. Army Corp of Engineers (1898)
Material: Shingled Wood Frame
Light Sequence: Red light - 6 second on, 6 second off - repeating
Fog Horn: No fog signal

Source: National Historic Register

National Register of Historic Places (12/07/1987)

Physical Appearance:

Situated at the southwest point of Arrowsic Island in the Kennebec River, the Squirrel Point Light Station is a relatively intact complex of five detached buildings. Wooden walkways link the keeper's house to two of these units.

The light tower at Squirrel Point is an octagonal wooden frame structure constructed in 1898 and covered in wood shingles. It is ringed by a narrow bracketed gallery (built in 1899) with a simple iron rail. The lantern houses a modern beacon, and a ventilator crowns the iron roof. Projecting from the west side is the small 1902 gable roofed bell house whose basement is sheathed in wood shingles. A door is located in the north side and a single six-over-six window punctuates the south wall.

A walkway and intervening modern deck connects the tower to the 1898 two-story keeper's house. This rather simply detailed dwelling is sheathed in replacement vinyl siding and capped by a cross gable roof. It has enclosed porches on both the north and south elevations and a brick flue rising through the roof.

Historical Significance:

The Squirrel Point Light Station is located on Arrowsic Island and the east bank of the Kennebec River. It is one of four river light stations constructed in 1898 as part of an integral system of navigational aids.

Federal recognition of the need for a system of navigational aids along the important Kennebec River waterway was expressed in the 1892 edition of the Annual Report of the Light-House Board. The Board proposed to establish four light stations including this one at Squirrel Point. In 1895 Congress authorized a $17,000 appropriation for this project, and the station was put into service three years later. It station was automated in 1982.

Additional Information

This lighthouse is located on Arrowsic Island on the Kennebec River, closest to the town of Arrowsic. It is the 2nd of four wooden frame lighthouses encountered when traveling north on the Kennebec River from Popham Beach to Bath. The lighthouse was named after the ship *HMS Squirrel*, which ran aground just off the island in 1717 with the royal governor of Massachusetts aboard.

Ownership of the light and surrounding structures has taken an interesting journey. In 1998, the 4.5 acre island was transferred by the Coast Guard to a man from Yarmouth, who formed a nonprofit organization, *Squirrel Point Associates, Inc*. The man hoped to establish an educational facility at Squirrel Point Light Station, but health problems got in the way and the property was put up for sale.

Meanwhile, a new group called *Citizens for Squirrel Point* formed to ensure that the light station would be used and maintained in accordance with federal, state, and local laws, as well as the covenants in the 1998 deed.

In 2003, the group filed suit in Federal district court to activate the reversion clause in Squirrel Point's deed on the grounds that Squirrel Point Associates had failed to honor these requirements. The court ruled in Citizens' favor and the Island was returned to the Coast Guard in 2005.

In 2008, the *Chewonki Foundation*, a Wiscasset environmental educational institution, signed a 15-year license to manage the light station property. However, the directors of the organization later decided that the lighthouse didn't fit into their plans, so the license was subsequently transferred to the original Plaintiff, Citizens for Squirrel Point. According to the group's website:

"Restoration of the keeper's house and shed is underway and will continue with generous support from gifts, grants, and volunteer efforts. Please join the effort to protect Squirrel Point Light and make a donation - any amount is greatly appreciated!" http://www.squirrelpoint.org/

Best Viewing

Squirrel Point Light can be accessed by a moderate to strenuous 2/3 mile hike from Bald Head Road in Arrowsic, or can be viewed from across the Kennebec River on Parker Head Road in Phippsburg.

Squirrel Point Light can also be viewed via boat tours in the area. As mentioned throughout this book, several popular lighthouse cruises are hosted by the Maine

Maritime Museum in Bath:
<https://www.mainemaritimemuseum.org/>

Among the cruises offered by the museum is the "Lighthouse Lovers Cruise," a 4 hour cruise that provides views of 10 of Maine's most iconic lighthouses: Doubling Point Light, Kennebec Range Lights, **Squirrel Point Light**, Perkins Island Light, Pond Island Light, Seguin Island Light, Cuckolds Light, Ram Island Light, Burnt Island Light, and Hendricks Head Light.

Squirrel Point Light is open to visitors one day per year on Maine Open Lighthouse Day. More information about this event can be found at:

<http://www.lighthousefoundation.org/maine-open-lighthouse-day>

16 Doubling Point Range Lights (Kennebec River Range Lights)

Year Established: 1898
Nearest to: Arrowsic
Latitude: 43° 52' 58" N
Longitude: 69° 47' 44" W
Tower Height (Front): 17ft
Tower Height (Rear): 13ft
Elevation (Front): 18ft
Elevation (Rear): 33ft
Design: Octagonal Tower
Designer(s): U.S. Army Corps of Engineers (1898)
Material: Shingled Wood
*Light Sequence (**Front**): white light – continuous quick light.*
*Light Sequence (**Rear**): white light – 6 seconds on, 6 seconds off - repeating*
Fog Horn: No fog signal

Source: National Historic Register

National Register of Historic Places (12/07/1987)

Physical Appearance:

The singularly unique Kennebec River Light Station consists of a pair of widely spaced octagonal frame light towers linked by walkways to a large two-story keeper's house. A brick oil house stands behind this dwelling. Formerly known as the Doubling Point Range Light, the twin towers are aligned in such a way so as to indicate the navigable channel in the Kennebec River.

Erected in 1898, both towers have a tapered octagonal shaft that is covered by a polygonal roof. The exteriors are sheathed in wood shingles. Entrances sheltered by shed hoods are located on one elevation of each tower. A small square window is positioned below the roof on the south, river elevation, and a smaller opening is positioned in the north side. The southernmost of the two towers stands seventeen feet in height from its granite base to the middle of the lens whereas the rear light is four feet shorter.

Historical Significance:

Located on Arrowsic Island a short distance to the east of the Doubling Point Light Station, the Kennebec River Light Station contains the only extant range lights in Maine. One of the four complexes built in 1898 along the Kennebec River, navigational aids along the Kennebec River had, prior to 1898, been maintained by private companies whose ships utilized the waterway. In 1892 the Annual Report of the Light-House Board recognized the need for improved, Federally operated lights. Three years later Congress appropriated $17,000 for a system of four light stations, one of which - the Kennebec River Light Station, was to contain a pair of range lights. This was put into service in 1898.

Additional Information

The Doubling Point Range Lights in Arrowsic are the 3rd of the four-station system erected along the Kennebec River in 1898.

The two lights mark an extreme double turn in the channel at Fiddler Reach where mariners line up the two lights to know they are on course. The lights are spaced a distance of 710 feet apart, with the rear light 15 feet higher than the front light, and are connected with a wooden walkway. Once the range lights were successfully navigated; ships could safety turn toward the Doubling Point Light, which was at this point visible upriver.

The original lights were upgraded to modern optics in 1979. The original rear tower light, a 5th order Fresnel, is now utilized at the Rockland Harbor Southwest Light as an active private aid to navigation.

In 1982, the range was consolidated into the Kennebec River Light Station, with one keeper for all four light stations along the river. The Doubling Point Range Lights were automated in 1990, making them among the last to be de-staffed in the United States.

In 1997, the light station was acquired by *The Range Light Keepers* http://www.rlk.org, a community based non-profit dedicated to the preservation of Doubling Point Range Lights.

Best Viewing

Doubling Point Range Lights can be seen from the end of Doubling Point Road in Arrowsic. The lighthouse grounds are open and accessible to the public. There is limited parking available. Follow paths to the towers and fog bell tower.

The keeper's house and light tower are open to visitors one day per year on Maine Open Lighthouse Day. More information about this event can be found at:

http://www.lighthousefoundation.org/maine-open-lighthouse-day

The light can also be viewed via boat cruises in the area. As mentioned throughout the book, several popular lighthouse cruises are hosted by the Maine Maritime Museum in Bath:

http://www.mainemaritimemuseum.org/

According to the Museum website:

Midcoast Lights and Rivers (3 hours)

*"On this cruise you'll see six lighthouses: Doubling Point Light, the **Kennebec Range Lights**, Squirrel Point Light, Perkins Island Light, Pond Island Light, and Seguin Island*

Light. Travel the winding Sasanoa River, and weather permitting, cruise the Sheepscot River past Hendricks Head Lighthouse."

17 Doubling Point Light

Year Established: 1898
Nearest to: Arrowsic
Latitude: 43° 52' 57" N
Longitude: 69° 48' 24" W
Tower Height: 23ft
Elevation: 23ft

Source: doublingpoint.org

Design: Octagonal Tower
Designer(s): U.S. Army Corps of Engineers (1898)
Material: Shingled Wood Frame
Light Sequence: White light – 4 sec. on - repeating.
Fog Horn: No fog signal

National Register of Historic Places (12/07/1987)

Physical Appearance:

Like the other Kennebec River lights built at the turn of the nineteenth century, Doubling Point Light Station consists of an octagonal wooden frame tower, a detached keeper's dwelling, a shed, and a brick oil house. The light tower, which stands offshore on a square granite base, is linked to the mainland by means of a three span wooden truss foot-bridge.

Erected in 1898, the tower is a tapered octagonal structure covered in wood shingles. A wooden walkway rings the tower off of which a door opens into the interior workroom. There is a single window in the north face and the bell support apparatus on the west side. A ladder rises to the bracketed iron walkway that is located below the octagonal lantern. Three granite piers support the foot-bridge.

Historical Significance:

The Doubling Point Light Station is situated on the west side of Arrowsic Island in the Kennebec River.

In 1892, the Annual Report of the Light-House Board carried a lengthy statement of the need for light and fog signals in the Kennebec River, gateway to the important harbor at Bath and the upriver communities of Gardiner, Hallowell and the state capitol at Augusta, the Kennebec River carried the traffic of 3,137 vessels in 1891 excluding daily passenger steamers. Based on these statistics, the Light-House Board requested appropriations for lights at Doubling Point, Squirrel Point, Perkins Island, and a set of range lights. It was not until 1895, however, that Congress appropriated the $17,000 needed for construction. In 1898 the system was completed and put into operation. Doubling Point light continues to provide an aid to navigation.

Additional Information

Furthest upriver of the four-station system erected in 1898, this light is located on the Kennebec River in Arrowsic. The first lighthouse keeper and his family stayed for 33 years. In total, there were only two keepers in the lighthouse's history.

In 1997, the light was transferred to the *Friends of Doubling Point Light* http://www.doublingpoint.org/

According to the Group's website *"Each spring, when the ice on the Kennebec River thaws, huge ice floes rush down the river in the swift current, and every few years, force the granite blocks that support the lighthouse tower further out of position. If reconstruction is not undertaken soon, the lighthouse will simply fall into the water. This disastrous destruction could occur any spring if the combination of wind, ice and tide is wrong."*

As a result of this plea, $50,000 was raised and the entire lighthouse tower was lifted from its base in 1999 so that the crumbling granite foundation could be repaired.

Best Viewing

As with the Doubling Point Range Lights, Doubling Point Light can be seen from the end of Doubling Point Road in Arrowsic. The lighthouse grounds are open and accessible to the public. There is limited parking available.

The keeper's house and light tower are open to visitors one day per year on Maine Open Lighthouse Day. More information about this event can be found at:

http://www.lighthousefoundation.org/maine-open-lighthouse-day

The light can also be viewed via boat cruises in the area. As mentioned throughout the book, several popular lighthouse cruises are hosted by the Maine Maritime Museum in Bath:
https://www.mainemaritimemuseum.org/

According to the Museum website:

Midcoast Lights and Rivers (3 hours)

"On this cruise you'll see six lighthouses: **Doubling Point Light***, the Kennebec Range Lights, Squirrel Point Light, Perkins Island Light, Pond Island Light, and Seguin Island Light. Travel the winding Sasanoa River, and weather permitting, cruise the Sheepscot River past Hendricks Head Lighthouse."*

***

18 Hendricks Head Light

Year Established: 1829
Nearest to: West Southport
Latitude: 43° 49' 21" N
Longitude: 69° 41' 23" W
Tower Height: 39ft
Elevation: 43ft
Design: Square Tapered Tower
1st Designer(s): Joseph Berry (1829)
2nd Designer(s): U.S. Army Corps of Engineers (1875)
Material: Brick
Light Sequence: Red or white light depending on heading – continuous
Fog Horn: No fog signal

Source: National Archives

National Register of Historic Places (10/13/1987)

Physical Appearance:

Hendricks Head Light Station is composed of a square tapered brick light tower connected to a large two-story keeper's house by way of a covered passageway. A second walkway leads to the bell tower and a frame shed and brick oil house stand to the northwest of the house. The present complex replaces the original 1829 structure that employed a rubble stone dwelling surmounted by a lantern.

The light tower and keeper's house, built in 1875, is similar in form to others built in Maine during the 1870s. A door, sheltered by the wood shingled covered passage, punctuates the north elevation below a six-over-six window. A second window is located on the tower's south side. The tower is capped by an iron deck with a railing. At the center of this deck is the octagonal lantern whose conical roof is crowned by a spherical ventilator. The covered walkway extends to a much longer passageway which at one end meets the house and at the other end is connected to the tapered bell that was built in 1890. The latter is supported by four iron posts and originally had a pyramidal skeletal frame.

When constructed in 1829, the light station consisted of a low one-and-a-half-story rubble stone cottage that was three bays in width. Mounted atop one end of the gable ridge was the polygonal tower. In 1875 this structure was pulled down and replaced by the present brick tower and frame keeper's house. The light was discontinued in 1933 and sold to W. Prichard and Mary L. Browne in 1935. In 1951 the Coast Guard recommissioned the light but the buildings remain in private ownership.

Historical Significance:

The Hendricks Head Light Station is a virtually intact complex whose design clearly illustrates the technological and architectural features of the early 1870s phase of lighthouse construction in Maine.

Located behind a shallow rock ledge on the east side of the mouth of the Sheepscot River, the light station at Hendricks Head was established in 1829 as a guide to Sheepscot River and the important harbor at Wiscasset. Incorporated in 1802, Wiscasset enjoyed a brief period of prosperity in the early nineteenth century resulting in large part from shipbuilding activities at its deep sheltered harbor and maritime commerce. Its sister settlements on the Sheepscot, including Southport, Cape Newagen and Hendricks Head, were also keenly dependent on the local fishing industry and later in the century on tourism.

Additional Information

In 1991, Hendricks Head Light was purchased by the owners of Russell Athletic Sportswear. In a description posted by the owners, *"The Russell's completely renovated each of the structures and by 1993, all were in near perfect condition. The fog bell tower has been restored to its original configuration, but remains inactive. Each structure is white except the 1895 red brick whale oil house and all buildings now have the typical bright red roofs. Today, the entire point reflects a rare picture postcard scene, reminiscent of a turn- of- the- century U.S. Light Station."*

http://benrussell.com/HH-home.htm

Hendricks Head Light is notable for the intensity of storms to hit the area. The lighthouse was featured in historian Edward Rowe Snow's book *"Famous Lighthouses of New England"* relating perhaps the best-known story involving a Maine lighthouse, a storm and wreckage that happened in March 1875.

In this story, a ship was observed in the distance wrecked against the rocks during a winter gale and the people on board were seen climbing the ship's rigging in a desperate attempt to survive. As night fell the keepers lit a bonfire but no survivors arrived. However, a bundle of feather beds was retrieved by the lighthouse keepers. Inside, a baby girl was found with a note entrusting her to the care of God. As the legend goes, the keepers, who had recently lost their own child, adopted the baby and named her Seaborne.

http://benrussell.com/HH-baby_that_washed_ashore.htm

Best Viewing

This light is located at the Sheepscot River entrance in Cozy Harbor, nearest to the town of West Southport.

The light can be viewed West Southport Beach or by area boat cruises.

As mentioned throughout this book, several popular lighthouse cruises are hosted by the Maine Maritime Museum in Bath: *https://www.mainemaritimemuseum.org/*

Among the cruises offered by the museum is the "Lighthouse Lovers Cruise," a 4 hour cruise that provides views of 10 of Maine's most iconic lighthouses: Doubling Point Light, Kennebec Range Lights, Squirrel Point Light, Perkins Island Light, Pond Island Light, Seguin Island Light, Cuckolds Light, Ram Island Light, Burnt Island Light, and **Hendricks Head Light**.

19 Cuckolds Light

Year Established: 1907
Nearest to: Southport
Latitude: 43° 46' 46" N
Longitude: 69° 39' 00" W
Tower Height: 48ft
Elevation: 59ft

Source: National Historic Register

Design: Octagonal Tower
Designer(s): Unknown (1907)
Material: Granite / Cast Iron
Light Sequence: White light – 1 second on, 1 second off, 1 second on, 3 second off – repeating
Fog Horn: 1 blast every 15 seconds

National Register of Historic Places (10/18/2002)

Physical Appearance:

The Cuckolds Light Station was established in 1907 at the previously established 1892 fog signal station. The fog signal station was completed on November 16, 1892, at a cost of $24,750 including all machinery in place. The only access to the island is by boat or helicopter.

The Cuckolds Light Station is located about 3/8ths of a mile south of Cape Newagan, Maine, on a barren rock ledge or island marking the ocean entrance to Boothbay Harbor. The rock is about 15 feet above high water at its highest point and is washed by the sea in heavy storms.

Therefore, a semicircular granite pier was constructed on the highest part of the island to support and raise the fog signal station structure above the storm waves. The light tower was later mounted on the fog signal building. This structure and the formerly existing keeper's quarters are located approximately in the center of the rock. The station cistern and storeroom were located inside the semicircular granite pier. The formerly existing boathouse was located on the northwest side of the island where it was partially protected by a smaller nearby island. The foundations of the boathouse are located at the end of the boat ways about 150 feet from the western edge of the island. The helicopter platform is located west of the fog signal station.

Historical Significance:

The Cuckolds Light Station is significant for its association with federal government's efforts to provide an integrated system of navigational aids and to provide for safe maritime transportation in the United States. The Cuckolds Island Light Station marks the entrance to Boothbay Harbor from the ocean. The station first served as a fog signal station in 1892, but, in 1907, a light tower was added. The historic integrity of the station has been compromised by the destruction of all the station structures except the fog signal building and light tower built upon it. Still, the fog signal structure is unique because of its granite pier construction built to protect the station from storm waves and its later modification to a light tower. The light and fog signal at the station continue as active aids to navigation.

Boothbay Harbor was a busy fishing port in the 19th and early 20th century. The barren rock upon which the Cuckold station is located was first marked by a wooden tripod daymark. Because the daymark was of little use at nighttime or in foggy weather, a fog signal station was established in 1892. A light tower was added to the station in 1907 due to increased fishing vessel traffic in the bay. The station was automated in 1975.

The Lighthouse Board Report for 1890 described the need for a fog-signal station at Cuckolds as follows:

> The Cuckolds consist of two rocky islets rising about 15 feet above high water in the westerly edge of the channel at the entrance to Booth Bay. The Atlantic Coast Pilot says of them:
>
> They are dangerous of approach on their southern side on account of the reefs in that direction, and the shoals also extend half a mile to the westward of the western rock, ...but the eastward side of the eastern rock is quite bold-to. The flood current sets right on these rocks.
>
> They are much dreaded by mariners in thick weather and are a great peril to a large number of vessels, as it is estimated that from three to four thousand enter the bay for refuge in Booth Bay Harbor, which is well protected and is one of the most useful and important harbors of refuge on the coast of Maine. It is therefore recommended that a fog-signal be placed on the Cuckolds of sufficient range to warn vessels of their approach. Numerous petitions have been received asking for the establishment of this fog-signal, and the Board, after careful investigation, has found that a fog-signal of sufficient range upon the easterly island of the Cuckolds will give vessels adequate warning of their approach and would be of great benefit to navigators. It is estimated that a keeper's dwelling, fog-signal house, cistern, bulkhead, machinery, etc., will cost $25,000, and an appropriation of this amount is recommended therefor.

There was limited room on the island so a wooden light tower was built upon the brick fog signal building. The light station was described in 1930 as consisting of 7 acres, more or less of rocks, with the following improvements: a dwelling and fog signal house surmounted by a tower, boathouse and slip, bulkhead. The land was valued at nothing and the improvements at $32,000.

Additional Information

Cuckolds Light was the final government-constructed light station in Maine, ending a 117-year period of creating these majestic structures.

The origin of the lighthouse's odd name may stem from the derisive term (cuckold) for a man whose wife was unfaithful, and was perhaps an exclamation shouted by mariners as they carefully navigated the two rocky inlets entering Boothbay Harbor that were "much dreaded by mariners and of great peril to a large number of vessels."

Another, more innocent theory was that The Cuckolds were named by an Englishman in honor of a point of land in southwest London along the Thames River known as "Cuckold's Point." Legend has it that this land was granted to a London man to assuage his anger after King John had an affair with his wife.

However the naming originated, ironically, the light station has been converted into a romantic inn for overnight guests. In May 2006, ownership of the lighthouse was transferred to the *Cuckolds Fog Signal and Light Station Council*, under the National Historic Lighthouse Preservation Act of 2000. The group undertook the rebuilding of the keeper's quarters in 2011and in 2014 opened an Inn in the former keeper's quarters.

The Inn at Cuckolds describes itself as "The perfect destination for romantic getaways and special occasions." The Inn is open during summer months: *https://innatcuckoldslighthouse.com/*

Best Viewing

Cuckolds Light is located near the Boothbay Harbor approach off of Cape Newagen, nearest to the town of Southport. This light can be viewed distantly from the town landing in Cape Newagen village but is better viewed by various boat cruises in the Bath/Southport/Boothbay Harbor area, such as *Cap'n Fish's Audubon Puffin & Scenic Cruises:*

https://www.mainepuffin.com/

This 3 hour cruise along the Kennebec River features seven of the ten lighthouses of Sagadahoc Bay: (Burnt Island, **Cuckolds**, Seguin Island, Pond Island, Perkins Island, Doubling Point, and Squirrel Point.)

***

20 Burnt Island Light

Year Established: 1821
Nearest to: Southport
Latitude: 43° 49' 30" N
Longitude: 69° 38' 24" W
Tower Height: 30ft
Elevation: 61ft
Design: Conical Tower
Designer(s): Unknown (1821)
Material: Rubblestone/Brick
Light Sequence: Red or white light, depending on heading – 6 sec. on – repeating
Fog Horn: One second blast every 10 seconds

Source: National Archives

National Register of Historic Places (12/17/1976)

Physical Appearance:

The light tower is of fieldstone, brick and cement construction, painted white, conical form, 15 feet diameter at base, 9' 9" diameter at parapet, 61 feet above mean high water.

The details of light are 375 mm Fresnel classical lens, 1000 watt lamp, characteristic is a flashing red, two white sectors every six seconds; 2 one second flash. The red sector has 2,380 candlepower with a twelve mile range; white sector has a 10,800 candle power with a range of 15 miles.

There is an FA 232 Fog Signal whose range is ½ a mile. The characteristic of the fog signal is a one second blast every ten seconds. Tower was built in 1821.

Historical Significance:

Burnt Island Light Station was built in 1821 on the west side of the entrance to Boothbay Harbor. Its purpose was the guidance of ships, the carriers of cargo destined for the development of industry and commerce, into Boothbay Harbor approximately 1 1/2 miles away. The mission and buildings are basically the same today.

In 1888, a dead angle was put into the lantern at Burnt Island Light to prevent ships from being wrecked on the rocks called the Cuckolds. About 1890 the light was changed from fixed white to fixed red with two white sectors covering the fairways into Boothbay Harbor. This made the dead angle unnecessary. Two years later, the light was changed to flashing red every five seconds with two white sectors to prevent confusion with the other lights near the entrance of Boothbay Harbor.

Additional Information

Burnt Island got its name from the habit of local farmers to burn vegetation from the island each year so that it could be kept clear for sheep grazing.

Many people believe that the Burnt Island Light is the most beautiful lighthouse on the entire Atlantic seaboard, with comments such as:

"The shining whitewashed tower stands in bold contrast to the backdrop of dark evergreens and offers a tacit but cheery welcome to the waterborne visitor."

In 1962, Burnt Island Light was the last lighthouse in New England to be converted from kerosene to electricity and in 1988 was one of the last lights in Maine to be automated.

In 1998, the light stations transferred to the Maine Department of Marine Resources:
https://www.maine.gov/dmr/education/burnt-island/index.html

In this setting, Burnt Island Light has become a State educational resource: *"Come learn about Burnt Island's history, visit its working lighthouse, explore its five-acre island, and/or participate in professional development training. Approximately one mile from the port of Boothbay Harbor, this historic site is an exceptional educational and recreational facility for teachers, school children, summer visitors and boaters. Burnt Island can only be reached by boat."*

Best Viewing

This light is located at the entrance of Boothbay Harbor and can be viewed from Capital Island Road in Southport.

The light is not typically accessible to the public, but during the summer months an educational program and lighthouse tour is offered. The tour departs twice a week from Pier 8 (42 Commercial St.) in Boothbay Harbor for a scenic 15-minute cruise Board aboard the *Novelty* to Burnt Island:

https://www.maine.gov/dmr/education/burnt-island/tours.html

Burnt Island Light is open to visitors one day per year on Maine Open Lighthouse Day. More information about this event can be found at:

http://www.lighthousefoundation.org/maine-open-lighthouse-day

***

21 Ram Island Light

Year Established: 1883
Nearest to: Boothbay Harbor
Latitude: 43° 48' 13" N
Longitude: 69° 35' 57" W
Tower Height: 35ft
Elevation: 39ft
Design: Cylindrical Tower
Designer(s): U.S. Army Corps of Engineers (1883)
Material: Granite Block Base/Brick Tower
Light Sequence: Red or white light, depending on heading – 6 seconds on, 6 seconds off - repeating
Fog Horn: 1 blast every 30 seconds

Source: National Archives

National Register of Historic Places (12/07/1987)

Physical Appearance:

Ram Island Light Station consists of a round two-stage light tower, a one-and-a-half-story frame keeper's house, an oil house, and a gable roofed fuel house.

The light tower stands on a rock outcropping, and it was originally linked to the main island by means of a long elevated walkway. The entire complex, with the exception of the oil house, was built in 1883.

The tower is composed of a tall, cylindrical quarry faced ashlar granite base surmounted by a brick shaft which is of a smaller diameter. A wide corbelled frieze band rises to the iron walkway and railing.

The polygonal lantern, which shelters a modern beacon, features clear glass panes in its upper half and iron panels below. Its iron roof is capped by a spherical ventilator. The landward side of the tower's brick stage is punctuated by a door which formerly opened off the walkway.

Historical Significance:

The Ram Island Light Station was established in 1883 as a guide to Boothbay Harbor. The need for a light station that would guide shipping in and around Boothbay Harbor was clearly evident by the nature of the commerce at this busy port.

As shown in the 1883-84 edition of the Maine State Year-Book Boothbay contained a broad range of mercantile establishments and manufacturers that relied upon maritime transportation. In addition, Boothbay was rapidly developing a summer tourist industry that supported no fewer than seven hotels and boarding houses. The village was linked by steamboats to Bath, Wiscasset, Augusta, Portland, and Boston. Ram Island Light Station was automated in 1965.

Additional Information

In colonial times, coastal farmers managed their sheep population by isolating the rams offshore. In fact there are more than 20 "Ram Islands" off the coast of Maine.

Ram Island Light, not to be confused with Ram Island Ledge Light farther south, is situated within a very rocky island group that includes Ram Island, Fisherman Island, Outer Heron Island, White Island, and Damariscove Island.

The area was so abundant with shipwrecks that it became linked with a multitude of ghost stories, usually consisting of apparitions that warned sailors of impending wrecks. Tales of strange lights, fires, lightning, along with various wandering souls were told by mariners that escaped certain doom just in the nick of time.

In 1980, the light station was offered to the town of Boothbay, who respectfully declined due to high maintenance costs.

In 1983, the keeper's house was slated to be destroyed when the *Grand Banks Schooner Museum Trust*, associated with the *Boothbay Railway Museum*, stepped in and leased the station from the Coast Guard. In 1998, the station was officially transferred to the Trust.

Eventually, the *Ram Island Preservation Society* *http://www.schoonermuseum.org/* was formed, and restored many of the island structures. This included the keeper's house, and in 2002, the previously demolished walkway from the shore to the lighthouse tower was reconstructed.

Best Viewing

Ram Island Light is located on Fisherman's Passage nearest the town of Boothbay Harbor, and is neither accessible to the public, nor easily visible from the mainland. A distant view is available from Ocean Point in Boothbay Harbor.

This lighthouse therefore is best viewed by boat cruises within the area. As mentioned throughout this book, several popular lighthouse cruises are hosted by the Maine Maritime Museum in Bath: *https://www.mainemaritimemuseum.org/*

Among the cruises offered by the museum is the "Lighthouse Lovers Cruise," a 4 hour cruise that provides views of 10 of Maine's most iconic lighthouses: Doubling Point Light, Kennebec Range Lights, Squirrel Point Light, Perkins Island Light, Pond Island Light, Seguin Island Light, Cuckolds Light, **Ram Island Light**, Burnt Island Light, and Hendricks Head Light.

***

22 Pemaquid Point Light

Year Established: 1827
Nearest to: Bristol
Latitude: 43° 50' 12" N
Longitude: 69° 30' 21" W
Tower Height: 34ft
Elevation: 79ft
Design: Conical Tower
1st Designer(s): Jeremiah Berry (1827)
2nd Designer(s): Joseph Berry (1835)
Material: Rubblestone
Light Sequence: White light – 6 sec. on - repeating
Fog Horn: No fog signal

Source: National Historic Register

National Register of Historic Places (02/22/1985)

Physical Appearance:

Pemaquid Point Light, spectacularly located on a high promontory with long dramatically sea grieved ledges running southwesterly for a third of a mile into the ocean, was built originally in 1827 and rebuilt in 1857 [sic].

The station consists of three structures, a stone light tower with attached keeper's quarters and a red brick bell tower. The light tower is 34 feet high, square in configuration, and stands 79 feet above sea level with an 11,000 candlepower automated light. The keeper's quarters; also of stone, is a one story, single gable building. The bell tower, a square brick structure, is 12 feet high.

Historical Significance:

One of the most dramatically located lights on the Maine coast, Pemaquid Point Light is an extremely important navigational mark between the entrance to

Johns Bay and Muscongus Bay. In spite of its location, it has been the scene of a number of tragic shipwrecks owing to the long ledge which runs southwesterly from its base.

In 1934 the keeper's house and surrounding land was given to the State and is now a state park with the dwelling having been converted into a lighthouse and maritime museum.

Of passing interest is the fact that on what is now the location of the lighthouse, hundreds of people stood on September 5, 1813, to witness the epic single ship action between the British brig Boxer and the United States brig Enterprise, only a short distance from shore, in which the former was defeated.

Additional Information

The name "Pemaquid" is said to have had its origins in an Abenaki word for "situated far out."

In 1934, Pemaquid Point Light became the first Maine lighthouse to be automated through the use of a "sun valve" system. This unique system used the sun's rays to control an acetylene valve that powered the lamp. By all accounts this system worked well until the light was electrified..

Source: U.S. Mint

Pemaquid Point is one of the most visited and famous lighthouses in Maine. The lighthouse draws over 100,000 visitors each year. Pemaquid Point was the first lighthouse to be commemorated on U.S. currency, appearing on the 2003 Maine quarter.

In 1940, the town of Bristol purchased all portions of the light station except the light tower. The tower was leased to the *American Lighthouse Foundation* in 2000 and is today managed by the *Friends of Pemaquid Point Lighthouse*.

The keeper's house contains an apartment which is available for vacation rentals.

Best Viewing

This lighthouse is located at the entrance of Muscongus and John Bay nearest to the town of Bristol. To reach the lighthouse, take Route 130 south from Bristol to Lighthouse Park at Pemaquid Point.

The lighthouse and museum are accessible to the public during summer months. A fee is charged for parking and admission.

https://www.thefishermensmuseum.org

Pemaquid Point Light is open to visitors one day per year on Maine Open Lighthouse Day. More information about this event can be found at:

http://www.lighthousefoundation.org/maine-open-lighthouse-day

***

23 Monhegan Island Light

Year Established: 1824
Nearest to: Monhegan
Latitude: 43° 45' 53" N
Longitude: 69° 18' 56" W
Tower Height: 47ft
Elevation: 178ft
Design: Conical Tower
1st Designer(s): Unknown (1824)
2nd Designer(s): Alexander Parris (1855)
Material: Brick
Light Sequence: White light – 15 seconds on - repeating
Fog Horn: No fog horn

Source: National Historic Register

National Register of Historic Places (12/03/1979)

Physical Appearance:

Monhegan Island Light, dating from 1824, is a well-preserved lighthouse and supporting buildings in a spectacular setting.

The lighthouse proper is a circular granite tower, forty-seven feet high with a parapet and light casing above. The walls of the tower are not parallel, sloping inward from the base, making the tower a truncated cone. The beacon consists of a flashing white light of 30-second interval, each flash being 2.8 seconds in duration. Attached to the south side of the tower is a small, gable-roofed brick entry-house, with a doorway beneath a low arch.

Historical Significance:

Probably familiar to Basque, Breton, Spanish and Portuguese fisherman in the late 15th century, Monhegan Island was recorded by John Cabot in 1498. One early visitor aptly described this lonely outpost as "a great island that was backed like a whale". The colorful and imaginative Capt. John Smith landed on Monhegan in 1614 and his account of the attractions of the island and its anchorage eventually led to settlement as early as 1625. Since 1674, there has been continuous population of the place based largely on a fishing economy.

Today, Monhegan supports a year round population of about 100 which climbs to over 300 in summer with the arrival of cottager-owning summer residents. The rich and unusual flora has been carefully guarded by careful control of the wild areas of the island so that the natural beauty is largely unspoiled.

By sealed-bid public auction held on June 1, 1962, these buildings were acquired by *Monhegan Associates, Inc.*, an organization formed in 1954 *"to preserve for posterity the natural wild beauty, biotic communities, and desirable natural, artificial, and historic features of the so-called 'wildlands' portions of Monhegan Island, Maine, and its environs, as well as the simple, friendly way of life that has existed on Monhegan as a whole"*.

Additional Information

According to legend, the name "Monhegan" originated from the Algonquian people and translates to "out-to-sea island." In 1824, a 30 foot rubblestone tower was erected on the island, with a rotating white and red beacon – thus becoming the first colored beacon on the Maine seacoast. Like most other early 17th century lighthouses, this structure quickly deteriorated and was razed and replaced in 1850 by a 36 foot conical granite tower designed by renowned lighthouse architect Alexander Parris.

At 178 foot, Monhegan Light has the 2nd tallest elevation of all Maine lights, a mere 2 foot lower than the 180 foot elevation of the Seguin Island Light.

In 1985, the structure was transferred to the Monhegan Historical and Cultural Museum Association:

https://monheganmuseum.org/the-museum-association/

Best Viewing

This light is located on Monhegan Island at the southern approach to Muscongus bay, nearest to the town of Monhegan. The light is not visible from the mainland but the island is accessible to the public via a 90 minute ferry.

Monhegan Boat Line: *https://monheganboat.com/*

The keeper's house contains a museum that is open from July through Sept. According to the museum website:

"When donations of materials related to Monhegan's rich and varied history were sought, generous islanders and visitors responded enthusiastically. Donations of photographs, documents, furniture, equipment, Indian artifacts, and memorabilia began to pour in, and continue to do so. Increasingly in recent years the Museum has received paintings and other art works by members of the art colony that has flourished on the island since 1890."

Monhegan Island Light is open to visitors one day per year on Maine Open Lighthouse Day. More information about this event can be found at:

http://www.lighthousefoundation.org/maine-open-lighthouse-day

***

24 Franklin Island Light

Year Established: 1807
Nearest to: Friendship
Latitude: 43° 53' 31" N
Longitude: 69° 22' 28" W
Tower Height: 45ft
Elevation: 57ft
Design: Conical Tower
1st Designer(s): Benjamin Beal, Duncan W. Thaxter (1807)
2nd Designer(s): Ezekiel D. Demuth (1831)
3rd Designer(s): Unknown (1855)
Material: Brick
Light Sequence: White light – 6 sec. on - repeating
Fog Horn: No fog signal

Source: U.S. Coast Guard

Lighthouse Appearance and History

Franklin Island Light is one of only ten Maine lighthouses which are not registered with the National Register of Historic Places.

Twelve-acre Franklin Island, at the entrance to Muscongus Bay, is about six miles from the town of Friendship and about midway between Pemaquid Point and Port Clyde. Maritime trade was booming in the early 1800s in the vicinity of Muscongus Bay and the St. George River, and many vessels were wrecked on the treacherous rocks near Franklin Island.

Congress authorized a lighthouse and keeper's house for the island in 1806, and the buildings were completed in early 1807. Contractors Benjamin Beal and Duncan W. Thaxter of Hingham, Massachusetts, constructed a wooden tower and adjacent dwelling. This fixed white light was 50 feet above mean high water.

The lighthouse and dwelling were rebuilt in 1831 by contractor Ezekiel D. Demuth. The new rubblestone tower was 31 feet high to the lantern deck, and the octagonal wrought iron lantern was fitted with 10 lamps and 13-inch reflectors.

In 1853, a report from the newly formed United States Lighthouse Board proclaimed the towers at both Franklin Island and Baker Island to be "entirely worthless," and the dwellings at both locations so old and leaky that they were unhealthy. An appropriation for $10,000 was requested from Congress for the rebuilding of both stations. Subsequently a 3rd, 45-foot-tall round brick lighthouse was erected at Franklin Island in 1855, along with a new wood-frame keeper's house.

The light was converted to automatic acetylene gas operation in 1933, using the same style "sun valve" as the one employed Pemaquid Point Light. Regrettably, during the automation work, all the buildings at the light station were demolished, except for the lighthouse tower and an 1895 oil house. Today, only the tower remains.

Franklin Island is now part of the Maine Coastal Islands National Wildlife Refuge:

https://www.fws.gov/refuge/Maine_Coastal_Islands/about/franklinisland.html

In 1999, the Coast Guard licensed Franklin Light Preservation Inc. to care for the lighthouse. The Coast Guard approved the rebuilding of a pier on the island and requested a helipad be constructed for emergency search and rescue operations. These improvements were added in 2001, but two years later, the state's Department of Environmental Protection ordered that the pier and helipad be removed to preserve the wildlife habitat. The preservation group had assumed that since the Coast Guard had jurisdiction over the property, no permit was needed. As it turned out, any structure erected in coastal wetlands requires a state permit, even those placed on federal lands.

Best Viewing

Franklin Island Light is located near Friendship in Maine's Muscongus Bay, approximately 5 miles from shore. Lighthouse and island are closed to the public.

Remote views of Franklin Island Light can be obtained from the Rachael Carson Salt Pond Preserve in New Harbor.

There are no boat tours offered on a regular basis. You will need to charter a boat out of Friendship or Tenant's Harbor to get out to the lighthouse from shore.

Off Route 130 in New Harbor, Hardy Boat Cruises, provides cruises out to Monhegan Island, puffin tours and seal watching, and coastal tours in the fall, which may pass by Franklin Island Lighthouse.

Occasionally, a cruise is put on by the American Lighthouse Foundation as part of the *Midcoast Maine Lighthouse Challenge*. This cruise usually provides nice close up views of the Franklin Island Light. The boat tour usually occurs before July 4th weekend:

http://www.lighthousefoundation.org/midcoast-lighthouse-challenge/

***

25 Marshall Point Light

Year Established: 1832
Nearest to: St. George
Latitude: 43° 55' 02" N
Longitude: 69° 15' 40" W
Tower Height: 31ft
Elevation: 30ft

Source: National Historic Register

Design: Cylindrical Tower
1st Designer(s): Unknown (1832)
2nd Designer(s): U.S. Army Corps of Engineers (1857)
Material: Granite Block Base/Brick Tower
Light Sequence: White light - continuous
Fog Horn: No fog signal

National Register of Historic Places (12/07/1987)

Physical Appearance:

The Marshall Point Light Station consists of a one-and-a-half-story gambrel roofed keeper's house, a granite oil house and a detached round granite light tower. Standing on a rock outcropping which is located below and away from the mainland, the tower is connected to the shore by means of a four span wooden walkway that is supported by three granite piers.

The light tower, built in 1857, is a slender structure which is twenty-four feet in height from its base to the focal plane of the original lens. Its landward face has a narrow attached entrance vestibule that is surmounted by the circular iron parapet. The polygonal lantern, which now shelters a modern beacon, features a base whose separate units contain coupled round arched panels. Extending from the tower to the shore is a four span wooden walkway, an as yet undated replacement of the original covered way. This remarkably well preserved structure is comprised of simple king post trusses supported by tapered granite piers.

The exact configuration of the Marshall Point Light at the time it was established is not as yet positively known. Subsequent descriptions in the Annual Report(s) of the Light-House Board indicate that the original dwelling was constructed of stone. The shape and location of the tower is unknown. In 1857 this tower was replaced by the existing structure. Nearly four decades later the keeper's house was rebuilt; a remarkably late survivor among the numerous Maine stations that originally featured stone dwellings.

Historical Significance:

Marshall Point Light Station, which stands at the eastern entrance to Port Clyde Harbor, was established in 1832 and partially rebuilt in 1857 and 1896.

Port Clyde is one of a number of small coastal communities along the Saint George peninsula whose nineteenth century economy was heavily dependent upon maritime pursuits. It's long established fishing industry was supplemented beginning in the 1830s by local ship building enterprises that survived to the turn of the century.

In addition, Port Clyde was the site of a commercial ice industry and the home of the South Saint George Guano and Oil Corporation, both of which had their beginnings in the mid-1870s. Building on its fisheries, a canned lobster plant was founded in the 1880s. All of these industries relied upon water borne transportation whose successful transit of the area was closely tied to the operation of the Marshall Point Light Station.

Additional Information

In 1990, the *St George Historical Society* opened the first floor of the keeper's house as a museum, open from Memorial Day to Columbus Day. This house was built in 1895 after lightning destroyed the prior dwelling, and is a unique late 19th century Colonial Revival with gambrel roof.

According to the museum website:

http://www.marshallpoint.org

"The Marshall Point Lighthouse Museum boasts the largest reference center of historical information on the Saint George peninsula. Come and view our extensive library on quarrying, lobstering and the history of the town of Port Clyde.

The Museum contains a host of information and a great array of lighthouse memorabilia and lobstering and quarrying tools."

The Town of St. George successfully applied for Marshall Point under the Maine Lights program, and ownership was transferred in June, 1998. The Coast Guard is now responsible only for operation of the light and fog horn.

Notably, a scene from the film "Forrest Gump" was filmed at the Marshall Point in 1993, where Forrest can be seen traversing the walkway leading to Marshall Point Light.

Best Viewing

The light and museum are a short walk from a public parking area on Marshall Point Road in Tenants Harbor. Parking is free but limited.

Marshall Point Light is open to visitors one day per year on Maine Open Lighthouse Day. More information about this event can be found at:

www.lighthousefoundation.org/maine-open-lighthouse-day

26 Tenants Harbor Light (Southern Island Light)

Year Established: 1857
Nearest to: Tenants Harbor
Latitude: 43° 57' 40" N
Longitude: 69° 11' 05" W
Tower Height: 27ft
Elevation: 69ft
Design: Conical Tower
Designer(s): U.S. Army Corps of Engineers (1857)
Material: Brick
Light Sequence: No light signal
Fog Horn: No fog signal

Source: National Archives

National Register of Historic Places (10/13/1987)

Physical Appearance:

The Tenants Harbor Light Station occupies a shallow plateau located on the east side of the Southern Island and at the approach to Tenants Harbor. A bold rock ledge rings the island and a low rock wall frames three of the four components of the complex. The station is composed of a one-and-a-half-story wooden frame keeper's house joined to a circular brick tower, a detached shed, an oil house, and a pyramidal bell house.

The tower and keeper's house at Tenants Harbor was built in 1857. Rising to a height of just over twenty-seven feet from its base to the center of the lantern, the cylindrical brick tower is punctuated by a pair of small windows on opposing sides and capped by an iron deck and railing. The ten-sided lantern is covered by a shallow roof with a spherical ventilator. A narrow brick workroom links the tower with the dwelling.

Like each of its contemporaries the keeper's house has not retained its original board-and-batten siding.

Now sheathed in clapboards, the dwelling features a pair of twentieth century gable roofed dormers and an original, gabled vestibule on the-front (north) elevation. A pair of, windows are located to the east of this vestibule. The short one-story wing attached to the west end of the house is an 1887 addition. This elevation also contains a later brick chimney and flue.

Historical Significance:

Tenants Harbor Light Station is an important example of an 1850s Maine lighthouse complex that retains its integrity of design, setting and association. It is composed of a cylindrical brick light tower connected to a one-and-a-half-story keeper's house and detached shed, oil house and replica bell house.

The light station at Tenants Harbor was established in 1857 in a continued effort to provide aids to navigation along the coast of Maine. Its location of the eastern side of Southern Island placed the complex at a strategic position, enabling it to guide ships through the two entrances to Tenants Harbor. The village of Tenants Harbor is the largest community in the Town of St. George, and is located at the head of a long harbor. The light station continues to emphasize the maritime heritage of the area where an active shipbuilding industry produced more than seventy schooners between 1820 and 1870. Many of these vessels were used to convey ice, stone, lime, and lumber from numerous places such as the nearby granite quarries at Long Cove and Clark's Island.

In 1933 the light station at Tenants Harbor was decommissioned and sold to a private individual.

Additional Information

In 1934, the light was discontinued, and the station was sold to a Rockland resident. In 1978, renowned artist Andrew Wyeth purchased the light station and converted to bell tower into an artist's studio. Andrew's son Jamie Wyeth, also an artist, inherited the property in 1990 and remains the owner today.

Tenants Harbor Light has appeared in a number of well-known paintings by Andrew and Jamie Wyeth, including "*Signal Flags*", "*Fog Bell*" and "*Iris at Sea*," painted by Jamie Wyeth to help raise funds for the Island Institute of Rockland. Also in Rockland, the *Farnsworth Art Museum* https://www.farnsworthmuseum.org is home to an extensive collection of paintings from the entire Wyeth family.

Best Viewing

The lighthouse is not visable from the mainland nor is it accessible to the public. It can only be viewed by boat. Monhegan Boat Line https://monheganboat.com offers a cruise departing from Port Clyde that sails past Tenants Harbor Light. From their website:

"Lighthouses have stood guard all along the rockbound Maine coast for more than two centuries. At night and in stormy weather, their beacons safely light the way for mariners. Even in fair weather, they are always a reassuring sight as they add their beauty to the scenery.

Come with us and let us show you an array of lighthouses, including Marshall Point, Whitehead, Two Bush Light, and **Southern Island.**"

***

27 Whitehead Light

Year Established: 1804
Nearest to: St. George
Latitude: 43° 58' 43" N
Longitude: 69° 07' 27" W
Tower Height: 41ft
Elevation: 75ft
Design: Conical Tower
1st Designer(s): Benjamin Beal/Duncan W. Thaxter (1804)
2nd Designer(s): Unknown (1831)
3rd Designer(s): Alexander Parris (undocumented 1852)
Material: Granite Block
Light Sequence: Green light – 5 sec. on – repeating
Fog Horn: Two blasts every 30 seconds

Source: National Historic Register

National Register of Historic Places (01/29/1988)

Physical Appearance:

The Whitehead Light Station is a complex of six detached structures and buildings consisting of a conical granite light tower, a brick oil house, a detached frame keepers' house, one shed and a fog signal building.

Standing to the east of the keepers' quarters is the light tower, an 1852 replacement of the original structure. Its curved granite blocks, punctuated by four small windows that illuminate the stair, rise in coursed levels to a narrow walkway that is ringed by a simple iron balustrade. The sixteen sided lantern, which houses a modern beacon, has an iron base and conical roof crowned by a spherical ventilator. Projecting from the east side of the tower is a small gable roofed brick service room. Added in 1891, it has a door framed by the gable and a single fifteen pane casement window on the south wall.

Historical Significance:

The Whitehead Light Station, which occupies Whitehead Island and marks the west entrance to Penobscot Bay, was established in 1804. It is the third oldest station in Maine.

Whitehead light occupies a strategic location along the shipping routes of the mid coast. Sited at the west side of Penobscot Bay it guides shipping toward the approach to the important coastal communities of Rockland, Camden, Belfast, and Searsport. During the nineteenth century these were busy commercial ports whose economic livelihood was for many decades virtually dependent on maritime transportation. The significance of this station is further demonstrated by its secondary sea-coast light classification and the fact that a steam powered fog signal was erected here in 1869-70. The station was automated in 1982.

Although documentary proof has not as yet been located, the design of the tower is nevertheless attributed to Alexander Parris (1780-1852). This conjecture is supported by the uncanny resemblance of this structure to the 1851 tower at Monhegan which the architect is known to have designed. Furthermore, the highly sophisticated nature of the granite structure typifies Parris's work at other Maine lights including Mount Desert and Saddleback Ledge.

Additional Information

Whitehead Light is located in Penobscot Bay at the western entrance to Muscle Ridge Channel nearest to the town of St. George.

For vessels approaching Penobscot Bay via the primary southwest route, there were two channels into the bay – Muscle Ridge Channel to the west and Two Bush Channel to the east.

Neither channel was perfect. Two Bush Channel took mariners safely into the middle of Penobscot Bay, but left them vulnerable to any weather that might arise. Muscle Ridge Channel was a more direct route, and carried mariners closer to shore, protecting them from easterly winds - but required them to navigate around many dangerous islands, reefs, and ledges.

Mariners favored the faster Muscle Ridge Channel. Despite the inherent risks, the protection from weather and the proximity to their destination outweighed the risks. Whitehouse Island Light, the 3rd lighthouse constructed in Maine, provided these mariners with important navigational assistance.

In 1996, the Coast Guard transferred ownership of the light station to Pine Island Camp, a non-profit group that has operated a boy's camp in Belgrade Lakes since 1902. Pine Island Camp had previously acquired 70 acres on Whitehouse Island in the 1950s.

Pine Island Camp subsequently installed an adult education program, with various onsite educational opportunities, and also schedules vacation rentals of the light keeper's house during the summer months. For more information: *http://www.whiteheadlightstation.org*

Best Viewing

Whitehead Light is located in Penobscot Bay at the western entrance to Muscle Ridge Channel nearest to the town of St. George. The lighthouse is not visible from the mainland and can only be accessed as part of the island's educational programs or vacation rentals.

Whitehead Light tower is also open to visitors one day per year on Maine Open Lighthouse Day. More information about this event can be found at:

www.lighthousefoundation.org/maine-open-lighthouse-day

Otherwise, the light is best viewed by boat. Monhegan Boat Line https://monheganboat.com offers a cruise departing from Port Clyde that sails past Two Bush Light. From their website:

"Lighthouses have stood guard all along the rockbound Maine coast for more than two centuries. At night and in stormy weather, their beacons safely light the way for mariners. Even in fair weather, they are always a reassuring sight as they add their beauty to the scenery.

Come with us and let us show you an array of lighthouses, including Marshall Point, **Whitehead***, Two Bush Light, and Southern Island."*

28 Two Bush Island Light

Year Established: 1897
Nearest to: Sprucehead
Latitude: 43° 57' 51" N
Longitude: 69° 04' 26" W
Tower Height: 42ft
Elevation: 65ft
Design: Square Tower

Source: U.S. Coast Guard

Designer(s): W. H. Glover Company (1897)
Material: Brick
Light Sequence: Red or white light, depending on heading – 4 sec. on – repeating
Fog Horn: One blast every 15 seconds

Lighthouse Appearance and History

Two Bush Island Light is one of only ten Maine lighthouses which are not registered with the National Register of Historic Places.

The island was named for its two lone pine trees, long since gone, that served as day markers before the 42-foot-tall square lighthouse was constructed. The light tower was originally painted brown, but was repainted white in 1917 to increase its visibility.

The light is located on the outer reaches of Penobscot Bay, a heavily traveled region due to its proximity to Bangor. By 1860, Bangor was a thriving lumbering and shipbuilding town. Nearby Rockland provided nearly all of the lime for plaster and mortar to New York City, and the area was also well known for its many granite quarries. Before the establishment of railroads, the only viable option for delivering this cargo to northeastern cities was via water.

As early as 1872, locals began requesting a light for Two Bush Island, to no avail. The same petition came before Congress again two years later, again with no action. The requests continued every few years. Finally, in 1892, the Lighthouse Board recognized the need for a light on Two Bush Island, and funds were appropriated for construction of the light station.

The Coast Guard automated Two Bush Island Light in 1964. For several years after this, Coast Guard keepers at nearby Whitehead Light Station operated the Two Bush Island fog signal and monitored the light remotely. An intercom system was installed so that the keepers at Whitehead Light could hear Two Bush's fog signal compressor running when they turned it on.

In 1969, the Coast Guard regrettably decided to raze the keeper's house. When all demolition submissions exceeded the budgeted amount, the Coast Guard allowed the 10th Special Forces Group from Massachusetts to blow up the dwelling in a training exercise. The blast leveled the residence, left cracks in the tower's brick walls and blew out several panes of glass.

Under the Maine Lights Program, the lighthouse became the property of the U.S. Fish and Wildlife Service in 1998. According to their website:

"Once essential for safe maritime travel, lighthouses now provide sanctuary for nesting seabirds. Eight lighthouse islands on the Maine coast have been transferred from the U.S. Coast Guard to the refuge."

https://www.fws.gov/refuge/Maine_Coastal_Islands/about/lighthouses.html

Best Viewing

The lighthouse is not visible from the mainland nor is it accessible to the public. It can only be viewed by boat. Monhegan Boat Line *https://monheganboat.com* offers a cruise departing from Port Clyde that sails past Two Bush Light. From their website:

"Lighthouses have stood guard all along the rockbound Maine coast for more than two centuries. At night and in stormy weather, their beacons safely light the way for mariners. Even in fair weather, they are always a reassuring sight as they add their beauty to the scenery.

*Come with us and let us show you an array of lighthouses, including Marshall Point, Whitehead, **Two Bush Light**, and Southern Island."*

***

29 Matinicus Rock Light

Year Established: 1827
Nearest to: Matinicus
Latitude: 43° 47' 00" N
Longitude: 68° 51' 18" W
Tower Height: 53ft
Elevation: 90ft

Source: U.S. Coast Guard

Design: Cylindrical Tower
1st Designer(s): Unknown (1827)
2nd Designer(s): Alexander Parris, Gridley Bryant (1847)
3rd Designer(s): Unknown (1857)
Material: Granite Block
Light Sequence: White light – 10 seconds on – repeating
Fog Horn: 1 blast every 15 seconds

National Register of Historic Places (1/29/1988)

Physical Appearance:

Matinicus Rock Light Station consists of a widely separated pair of cylindrical granite towers, only one of which remains active. A rectangular frame and granite keeper's house is connected to the functioning light tower. Extant ancillary structures include a frame shed and boathouse.

Rising to a height of forty-one feet from its base to the middle of the lantern, the southmost of the two towers is an ashlar granite structure whose shaft is capped by a narrow circular walkway. It was built in 1857. Framed by an iron railing, this walkway is surmounted by a short round brick stage punctuated by a row of bulls-eye windows. The twelve-sided lantern, which is glazed from its base to the polygonal roof, is surmounted by a spherical ventilator. A winding iron stair extends from the base of the tower to the brick stage. A short, narrow brick workroom connects the tower to the keeper's house.

Standing 180 feet to the north of the active tower is the granite base of the second tower, also erected in 1857. Similar in design to its counterpart but originally taller, this structure has lost its lantern room, workroom and frame board-and-batten assistant keeper's house. Documentary photographs show that a long covered passageway originally linked this tower to the main granite dwelling.

Historical Significance:

Occupying a lonely island off the south end of Matinicus Island, the Matinicus Rock Light Station was established in 1827 and substantially rebuilt in 1847 and 1857. Originally classified as a primary seacoast light (a designation changed to secondary seacoast light by 1886), this station is of particular importance as a guide along the coastal shipping lanes off the southern entrance to Penobscot Bay.

Matinicus Rock Light Station was the fourteenth such complex established along the Maine coast. At the time of initial construction it was the most distant light from the mainland and the first one to employ a pair of towers. These were located at the ends of the original rectangular rubble stone keeper's house with wooden towers.

The 1847 rebuilding resulted in the construction of the existing granite dwelling and twin towers again located at each end of the house. Ten years later new towers were designed and placed 180 feet apart.

The importance of the station as well as the inclement weather is further demonstrated by the fact that a steam fog signal was established here in 1869 making it one of the few such devices put into service in Maine at this early date.

After the 1857 reconstruction the complex at Matinicus was continually enlarged and transformed through the addition and removal of a host of ancillary buildings such as dwellings, rain sheds and cisterns. Beginning in the 1950s, however, many of these buildings and structures have been pulled down as new aids to navigation have made these components obsolete. In 1983 the station was automated.

Additional Information

Matinicus is an Abenaki word meaning "far out island." Matinicus Rock, not to be confused with the much larger Matinicus Isle, is a 32 acre rock outcropping located 25 miles southeast of Rockland, making it Maine's furthest lighthouse out to sea.

Protecting the outer reaches of Penobscot Bay, as well as ships travelling along the coast, the Matinicus Rock Light originally housed two lights. These were the first "ranging lights" constructed in Maine. The distance between the lights, when viewed from sea, helped determine the position of vessels traveling past the lights.

Originally, in 1827, two wooden light towers were placed on either end of a stone keeper's house. These structures were replaced in 1845 by noted lighthouse architect Alexander Parris. The new granite towers used the same placement as the original and were located on either end of the keeper's house

Ten years later, Parris' towers were replaced, not because they were poorly built, but because mariners complained that the lights easily merged into one light, making it difficult for them to establish their position.

As a result, in 1855 the Lighthouse Board directed that a new pair of granite lighthouse towers should be spaced 180 feet apart, so that probability of them merging into a single light when seen from the sea was lessened.

Under the Maine Lights Program, the lighthouse became the property of the U.S. Fish and Wildlife Service in 1998, where Puffins and other seabirds are now studied. According to their website:

"Once essential for safe maritime travel, lighthouses now provide sanctuary for nesting seabirds. Eight lighthouse islands on the Maine coast have been transferred from the U.S. Coast Guard to the refuge."

https://www.fws.gov/refuge/Maine_Coastal_Islands/about/ligh thouses.html

Best Viewing

Matinicus Rock Light is located approximately five miles south of Matinicus Isle in Penobscot Bay, nearest to the town of Matinicus.

The outcropping is maintained as a bird sanctuary with nesting colonies of puffins, and has very limited public access.

This light cannot be seen from the mainland and can only be viewed by boat cruises in the area. One such cruise, Matinicus Excursions, offers water taxi and ferry service from the mainland to Matinicus Isle, as well as trips to Matinicus Rock Light:
http://www.matinicusexcursions.com/

30 Owls Head Light

Year Established: 1825
Nearest to: Owls Head
Latitude: 44° 05' 32" N
Longitude: 69° 02' 38" W
Tower Height: 26ft
Elevation: 100ft
Design: Cylindrical Tower
1st Designer: Unknown (1825)
2nd Designer: Unknown (1852)
Material: Brick
Light Sequence: White light – continuous
Fog Horn: Two blasts every 20 seconds

Source: National Archives

National Register of Historic Places (05/03/1976)

Physical Appearance:

Dwelling was built in 1826, 34' x 21', 2 story with attached shed, wood frame construction, painted white with green trim. Storage Building was built in 1826, 11' x 10' x 9' high, brick with shingle roof.

Light Tower was built in 1826, brick, 14' diameter, 30' high, round, painted white. A bronze plaque was placed on the light by the Mussel Historical Society on July 21, 1962. The town of Owls Head has a park named "Lighthouse Park" on the land adjacent to the light station.

The light on the tower is a fourth order, fresnel cut glass lens protected by rectangular storm panes projecting a fixed, white beam, candle power 20400, 16 mile range, focal plane at high water, 100 feet.

The fog signal on the light tower is an ELG 300/02 with a range of 4 miles.

Historical Significance:

The lighthouse at Owl's Head designates the entrance to Rockland Harbor, Maine.

The ships that were guided to safe harbor by the light carried the goods, raw material and people that assisted in the development of coastal villages to modern towns and cities of today. Ships and boats were the main mode of transportation, and the sea, rivers and streams were the only roads.

The following history of the Owls Head Light consists of extracts from "*The Lighthouses of New England*" written by Edgar Rowe Snow.

At the entrance to the attractive seaport of Rockland, Maine is a high, wave-swept promontory, visible to all who sail up or down Penobscot Bay. Pine trees and grassy terraces vie with each other for possession of this rocky headland, while at the very peak of the cliff, partly surrounded by spruce trees, is a lighthouse.

The owl's head which gives the promontory its name is easily identified in the rocky cliff by the two cave-like hollows which form the eyes and a ridge which makes the bridge of the owl's nose. Rocks that jut out on either side of the bridge form two eyeballs.

Schooners from Owl's Head made voyages to Europe, delivering shipments of lime and returning with cargoes of salt. Sail after sail passed the attractive Maine promontory, but many of them were wrecked in fog and storm before they made port. Agitation started for the erection of a lighthouse, and when in 1823 the steamer *Maine* made regular stops at Owl's Head, plans were developed to build a light high on the nearby headland.

In September 1825, Owl's Head Light was illuminated for the first time. The granite tower had been built at the highest peak of the promontory, eighty-two feet above the sea, with the focal point of the light one hundred feet above the water.

One of the strangest events in the entire history of Maine took place between Owl's Head and Spruce Head in the year 1850. During the terrible December 22 gale of that year five vessels were thrown ashore between the beach at Owl's Head and Spruce Head, about eight miles away.

The weather was far below zero that night, and spray froze on each of the five wrecked ships until they were encased in ice several inches thick. A coasting schooner, owned by Henry Butters of Haverhill, had been anchored off Jameson's Point when the storm broke. Aboard the schooner were three persons, the mate, his bride-to-be, and a deck hand.

The schooner's cables snapped sometime before midnight and the vessel was pushed across the harbor by the terrific winds and waves, finally being thrown with great force against the cruel ledges just off Spruce Head. Although she filled at once, the schooner did not sink as the rocky cradle where she hit held her, her decks just above water.

Down below, the girl had already retired for the evening, but when the schooner crashed, the young woman grabbed a large blanket and hurried up on deck. The three frightened people huddled in the shelter of the taffrail. Every monstrous wave that roared in at them out of the storm left its covering of spray, which soon froze into solid ice. Something had to be done at once, or they would all perish.

The mate then thought of a plan. Making the girl lie down next to the taffrail, he lay down beside her and then covered her with the blanket. The deck hand crawled in beside the mate, and the blanket was pulled over so that all three were under its protection. The bitter night wore on. The tide rose higher and higher, until every single wave broke directly across the schooner.

Then the tide started to turn and go out, and as morning came, the deckhand, who had kept hacking with his sheath knife to keep a small air hole open through the thick ice, took heart. Striking and slashing at the heavy icy covering that had entombed him with his two companions, at times using his bleeding hands as clubs, he chopped and punched his way out from under the ice cap that had built itself up over the three shipwrecked victims.

Without question, the heavy woolen blanket had saved his life. It was then six o'clock in the morning. After resting a few moments from the strenuous exertions of escaping from the ice cap, the sailor crawled to the rail nearest shore, clambered over the side, and dropped to the icy rocks below. Working his way on hands and knees, he finally reached the high-tide mark, and then collapsed from exhaustion.

It was still below zero, so he forced himself to get up and continue his efforts. Foot by foot, yard by yard, the bruised and bleeding man fought his way through the heavy drifts of snow that lined the shore. Now falling, now upright, the sailor made steady progress inland, until finally he reached a road.

In the distance he saw a pung driven by the keeper of Owl's Head Light coming slowly his way. Knowing that he was to be saved, he fell across the highway in a dead faint. Brought to the keeper's home, the sailor was quickly revived and asked to tell his story. When the keeper and his family realized that the boy and girl were still aboard ship under the heavy blanket and several inches of ice, they made plans to reach the schooner.

Retracing the sailor's steps in the snow, the members of the rescue party were soon able to see the masts of the schooner showing above the snowdrifts. A short time later several of the rescue party boarded the schooner. Guided by the directions given them, they arrived at the taffrail where the two lovers were encased in the ice.

Chopping and cutting around their forms, the men soon were able to lift the frozen pair up from the deck, although it was agreed that they had probably frozen to death. The boy and girl were carried over the side and handed down to others waiting below. The rescuers decided that an effort should be made to revive them. Within a half hour they were taken to a home where they were treated with application of cold water.

At first the water's temperature was almost freezing, and then it was gradually raised until it reached approximately fifty five degrees. Next the hands and feet of the two frozen people were slowly raised and lowered, and their bodies ceaselessly massaged.

The girl was the first to awaken from her deathlike sleep, stirring slightly after two hours' attention. Her lover took almost a full hour more to respond to the steady treatment, but he finally showed signs of life, and a few moments later actually opened his eyes.

Both were covered with warm blankets and made to rest. Several weeks elapsed before they were able to get up and walk, but when spring came they had almost completely recovered. The following June their marriage took place. The story of their strange experience was told up and down the Maine coast for many generations.

The deckhand fared worse, however. Whether it was from his more exposed position, or because of his efforts in reaching help, he never fully recovered from his terrifying experiences that bitter December night in 1850. He did not go to sea again, but became a well-known figure on the local waterfront.

Additional Information

In 1989, Owls Head Light became the last lighthouse in the state of Maine to be automated, ending a 200-year legacy of onsite light station keepers.

In 2007, the Coast Guard leased the light tower to the *American Lighthouse Foundation*, who undertook extensive renovation in 2010. In 2012, the keeper's house was also leased to the Foundation, who utilizes it for its offices and an interpretive center.

Best Viewing

This light is located in West Penobscot Bay at the entrance to Rockland Harbor, nearest to the town of Owls Head. The lighthouse is located within Owls Head State Park, located at the end of Lighthouse Road.

The grounds are accessible and open to the public. The tower is managed by the Friends of Rockland Harbor Lights, and is open to the public on weekends during tourist season: *http://www.rocklandharborlights.org*

Owls Head Light is open to visitors one day per year on Maine Open Lighthouse Day. More information about this event can be found at:

www.lighthousefoundation.org/maine-open-lighthouse-day

Of special note, Owls Head Light was rated *the most haunted lighthouse* by *Coastal Living* magazine:

https://www.coastalliving.com/travel/top-10/top-10-haunted-lighthouses

***

31 Rockland Breakwater Harbor Light

Year Established: 1902
Nearest to: Rockland Harbor
Latitude: 44° 06' 14" N
Longitude: 69° 04' 39" W
Tower Height: 25ft
Elevation: 39ft
Design: Square Tower
Designer(s): W.H. Glover Company (1902)
Material: Brick
Light Sequence: White light – 5 sec. on – repeating
Fog Horn: One blast every 15 seconds

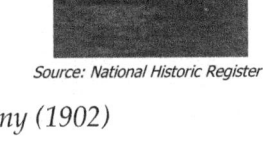

Source: National Historic Register

National Register of Historic Places (11/17/1980)

Physical Appearance:

The Rockland Breakwater Lighthouse, located at the end of a 4,300-foot breakwater, is a well-preserved structure with associated buildings. The complex, completed in 1902, consists of the lighthouse itself, a fog-signal building, and a Keeper's house, all constructed on a rectangular platform of dressed granite. All of these elements are attached to each other, and indeed the lighthouse tower rises from the roof of the fog signal building.

The fog-signal building and the lighthouse tower are of brick construction, and the former has a gable roof with cornice returns covering its 1 1/2 stories. The tower, square in plan, has a projecting iron balcony on all four sides at roof level, providing access to the light itself.

The Keeper's house is a gambrel-roofed building of frame construction, with 1 1/2 stories, one central brick chimney and one exterior end chimney, and white-painted shingle siding. Fenestration is 6/6 and the facade is 5 bays wide. In the half-story on both the facade and rear of the house is a pair of gabled dormer windows.

Historical Significance:

The Rockland Breakwater Lighthouse marks the entrance to Rockland Harbor and as such is an important navigational aid. With the completion of the breakwater and the construction of the lighthouse in 1902, this became one of the finest harbors in Maine as befitted this thriving turn of the century commercial center. The breakwater has also been for many years a favorite tourist attraction.

The breakwater comprised of nine sections was laid between April of 1881 and November of 1899. At its outer extremity the Rockland Breakwater is 43 feet wide at the top and 175 feet wide at the base. Its height is 65 feet. Stone necessary for the entire project totaled 697,627 tons. The nine sections of this project was designed and engineered by the Army Corps of Engineers. Colonel George Thorn engineered the first section of the breakwater and reported on the possibilities of the entire project to the chief of Army Engineers. The soundings and plans allowed the various engineers who designed the sections to work with some continuity.

W.H. Glover Company erected the stone tower and accompanying dwelling which stand at the southern end of the breakwater. The lighthouse was lit in 1902 and was occupied by two keepers from the United States Coast Guard. In 1964 the Rockland Breakwater Lighthouse was automated by the Coast Guard.

Additional Information

Between 1881 and 1899, a 4,346 foot granite breakwater (eight-tenths of a mile) was built to help protect Rockland Harbor from strong nor'easters. The Bodwell Granite Company used approximately 700,000 tons of granite to construct the breakwater.

Once completed, the breakwater itself became a hazard to navigation, so in 1902, the current light tower and keeper's house were placed atop the ocean end of the breakwater, where it is 65 feet deep, 43 feet wide at the top, and 175 feet wide at the bottom. This light station permanently replaced several temporary light structures that were used as the breakwater was constructed.

After automating the light in 1965, the Coast Guard indicated their desire to demolish the entire light station. A public outcry ensued, and after the City of Rockland turned down the property, the Somoset Resort, located at the shore end of the breakwater, received a lease from the Coast Guard and assumed some responsibility for maintaining the structures.

In 1989, Samoset Resort gave up their lease and the light reverted back into the government's hands. Surprisingly, the Coast Guard extensively refurbished the station in 1990.

In 1998, Rockland Breakwater Light was deeded to the City of Rockland. While officially owned by the City, the light station is under the direction of the American Lighthouse Foundation and managed by their local chapter - Friends of Rockland Harbor Lights.

Best Viewing

Rockland Breakwater Light is located on Samoset Road in Rockland. The breakwater is open to the public, but can be a hazardous walk during inclement weather.

The light tower is managed by the Friends of Rockland Harbor Lights, and is open to the public on weekends during tourist season: *http://www.rocklandharborlights.org*

32 Rockland Southwest Harbor Light

Year Established: 1987
Nearest to: Owls Head
Latitude: 44° 06' 26" N
Longitude: 69° 06' 28" W
Tower Height: 44ft
Elevation: 44ft
Design: Square Tower
Designer(s): Dr. Bruce Wollett
Material: Wood
Light Sequence: Yellow light - flashes once every 2.5 seconds
Fog Horn: No fog signal

Source: lighthousefriends.com

Lighthouse Appearance and History

Rockland Southwest Harbor Light is one of only ten Maine lighthouses not listed in the National Register of Historic Places, and the only privately built lighthouse in Maine that has been approved by the Coast Guard as an official aid to navigation. After being completed and equipped with a lens, the lighthouse was recognized as a private aid to navigation marking nearby Seal Ledge.

Because of the private nature of this light, not much is known about the design and construction of the tower and dwelling, nor the reasons which lead to the construction of this site.

What is known is the that a fifth-order Fresnel lens previously used at Doubling Point Range Lights was acquired and installed in the lighthouse in 1989, replacing the original copper lantern.

In 1998, the light station was sold to a new owner, who embarked on an extensive renovation of the lighthouse and grounds.

Best Viewing

This lighthouse is located near Rockland Harbor, nearest to the town of Owls Head. This light is privately owned and is not accessible to the public but a partially obscured view can be obtained from Shearmans Road in Owls Head.

The following information was obtained at the website *http://www.cyberlights.com*:

"The Rockland Harbor Southwest Light is located at the end of Shearmans Lane in Owls Head. The owner is not always friendly, but if people want a closer look without bothering the owner they are welcome to go to the beach in front of the lighthouse by using a beach path directly beside it that I own and park at the head of the trail. Happy Lighthousing everyone."

33 Indian Island Light

Year Established: 1850
Nearest to: Rockland
Latitude: 44° 09' 56" N
Longitude: 69° 03' 56" W
Tower Height: 37ft
Elevation: 53ft

Source: National Archives

Design: Square Tapered Tower
1st Designer(s): Unknown (1850)
2nd Designer(s): U.S. Army Corps of Engineers (1875)
Material: Brick
Light Sequence: No light signal
Fog Horn: No fog signal

National Register of Historic Places (12/21/1987)

Physical Appearance:

The Indian Island Light Station is composed of a detached tapered brick tower, a one-and-a-half-story T-shaped keeper's house, an oil house, and a pair of frame ancillary buildings. Now privately owned, the tower no longer carries a navigational aid.

Indian Island's light tower, built in 1874-75, bears the distinctive square tapered shape typical of the 1870s. Its brick walls are punctuated by a door and window on the south elevation and a single opening on both the east and west walls. A small gabled brick workroom with a door and two windows projects from the south side.

The tower is surmounted by a square iron walkway and railing. At the center of this platform is the octagonal steel lantern crowned by a spherical ventilator. This tower replaced the original light mounted atop the dwelling.

Historical Significance:

Indian Island Light Station was established in 1850. Situated on the west side of Indian Island, the light marked the entrance to Rockport Harbor.

At the time of its initial construction in 1850 the Indian Island Light Station was the principal aid to navigation in and around Rockport Harbor. The well sheltered and deep harbor at Rockport was a principal reason for the community's development. Known in the first half of the nineteenth century for its ship building activities, Rockport was later the center of an important lime industry (see the Rockport Historic Kiln Area, NR 1/27/70), as well as assorted commercial enterprises including ice harvesting and shipping.

The light on Indian Island was originally exhibited from a lantern mounted on the present brick dwelling. However, prior to the publication of the 1861 Light List the station was deactivated for an as yet unknown reason. In 1874 an appropriation was made to reestablish the light, and on January 15, 1875, the rebuilt complex was put back into service. The station served for nearly sixty years thereafter until it was sold in 1932.

Additional Information

Throughout the 1800s Rockport, named for its nearby rock quarries, processed limestone in kilns that operated around the clock. The lime that was produced was an important ingredient in building construction among eastern cities.

Seven-acre Indian Island, off Beauchamp Point at the east side of the entrance to the Rockland Harbor, received its name because local Native Americans took refuge on the island during the French and Indian War.

After the original lighthouse was constructed in 1850, it was deemed unnecessary by the Coast Guard in 1859, and deactivated. However, due to Rockport's flourishing lime and ice industries, the Coast Guard reconsidered their decision and in 1874 the Lighthouse Board announced that the light would go back into service with a new 37 foot brick tower. The light was permanently deactivated in 1934 when the lime industry declined in the area. That same year, the lighthouse was declared surplus and sold at auction in September 1934 for $1,025 to a Chicago resident. The property remains within the family's hands to this day.

Best Viewing

Indian Island Light is located in Rockport Harbor within Penobscot Bay, nearest to the town of Rockland. It is privately owned and not accessible to the public. It can be viewed distantly from Pascals Ave. in Rockland at the entrance to Rockport Marine Park.

The 65 foot Schooner *Heron* also provides an educational sail around Indian Island, departing daily during the summer. For more information:

https://sailheron.com/maine-schedule/

***

34 Curtis Island Light

Year Established: 1836
Nearest to: Camden
Latitude: 44° 12' 04" N
Longitude: 69° 02' 55" W
Tower Height: 25ft
Elevation: 52ft
Design: Cylindrical Tower
1st Designer: George Galilt (1836)
2nd Designer: Unknown (1896)
Material: Brick
Light Sequence: Green light – 4 sec. on – repeating
Fog Horn: No fog signal

Source: National Historic Register

National Register of Historic Places (05/05/1973)

Physical Appearance:

Curtis Island Light is located at the southern entrance to Camden Harbor. The island is approximately 4/5th of a mile from the town docking facility at Camden. The island itself is approximately 5 ½ acres with softwood dominating the foliage. The lighthouse is at the southern end of the island and the docking facility is at the northern end.

There are four structures on the island which are all part of the lighthouse facility. The light tower itself is of brick as is the small building housing the station's power supply. There is a tool shed or garage which is constructed of wood. The keeper's house is a one story frame house also constructed of wood and sheathed in clapboards. These structures are all at the southern end of the island.

From the island, one has an excellent view of one of the most scenic areas in Maine. The harbor, with the mountains in the background, form perhaps the most perfect harbor in Maine.

Historical Significance:

Curtis Island Light, or Negro Island Light, as it was called for one hundred years, was first built in 1836 under the presidency of Andrew Jackson. The light was built by George Galilt of Boston and the first keeper was H. K. M. Bowers. Bowers stayed on until 1841 and since then many men have occupied the position.

The light station must have fallen into disrepair at some time for in 1896 it was ordered rebuilt by President Grover Cleveland. For many years the island was a signal station for the Boston-Bangor boats, many of which stopped at Camden. This small island also served as a pleasure spot for many of Camden's residents and visitors as a favorite picnic area.

In 1934 the town of Camden honored one of its most distinguished summer residents, Mr. Cyrus H. K. Curtis, famous publisher and philanthropist.

The name of the island was changed from Negro Island to Curtis Island, Mr. Curtis was one of the island's many visitors each year. As a philanthropist, Mr. Curtis did much for the town of Camden so the citizens honored his name. His daughter, Mrs. Mary Louise Bok officiated at the dedication ceremony on August 6, 1934.

The island is a natural shelter for Camden Harbor in its function as a natural breakwater. It absorbs the fierce waves from the ocean while the harbor remains quite calm at all times.

The Curtis Island Lighthouse has for nearly one hundred and fifty years served the people of Maine who have eked a livelihood from the sea as a beacon of friendship and safety.

Additional Information

Curtis Island Light is located at the entrance to Camden Harbor, nearest to the town of Camden.

In 1970, word spread that the Coast Guard was planning to auction the light station, except for the tower. Three Camden residents traveled to Philadelphia for a meeting and managed to convince the Coast Guard that the station should go to the Town of Camden rather than to a private party.

Subsequently, when the light was automated in 1972, the town of Camden gained control of the island. In 1998, under the Maine Lights program, the town officially purchased the light station.

Best Viewing

Curtis Island is a public park but is accessible only by boat. The lighthouse is occasionally open to the public. The light can also be seen from the Curtis Island Overlook, on Bayview Street in Camden, just southeast of the intersection with Beacon Street.

You can get a panoramic view of Camden Harbor and Curtis Island by driving or hiking to the top of Mount Battie in Camden Hills State Park.

To reach Curtis Island, you'll need a rowboat or kayak for the 20 minute paddle across the harbor from the Camden Public Landing. Kayak rentals are available from *Ducktrap Kayak* in Lincolnville; they will even deliver your kayak to you: *http://ducktrapkayak.com/*

Guided kayak tours around Curtis Island are also available from Breakwater Kayak in Rockland: (

http://www.breakwaterkayak.com/

Curtis Island Light is open to visitors one day per year on Maine Open Lighthouse Day. More information about this event can be found at:

http://www.lighthousefoundation.org/maine-open-lighthouse-day

35 Grindle Point Light

Year Established: 1851
Nearest to: Isleboro
Latitude: 44° 16' 54" N
Longitude: 68° 56' 34" W
Tower Height: 39ft
Elevation: 39ft

Source: National Historic Register

Design: Square Tapered Tower
1st Designer(s): Unknown (1851)
2nd Designer(s): Unknown (1875)
Material: Brick
Light Sequence: Green light – 4 sec. on – repeating
Fog Horn: No fog signal

National Register of Historic Places (02/12/1987)

Physical Appearance:

Facing southwest across West Penobscot Bay, the Grindle Point Light Station is a virtually intact example of a square-towered lighthouse complex. It consists of a relatively short tapered brick light tower connected by a covered, below-ground passage to the frame keeper's house. The tower is capped by a steel deck which extends beyond the walls. This deck is partially supported by a curved steel cornice, and it has a perimeter iron railing. At the center of the deck is the lantern. The lens was removed from the tower before the site was sold to the Town of Islesboro in 1935. Four windows illuminate the circular staircase located within the structure.

The low gable roof covered passage located between the light tower and the dwelling is built on the foundation from the original 1850 structure. It has a single dormer on both the west and east facades.

Oriented with its steeply pitched gable roof perpendicular to the connecting passage, the keeper's house is one-and-a-half stories in height and an irregular three bays wide. It is covered in clapboards. The house features two windows and a door on the front (east) elevation and two windows in the second story. This fenestration pattern, less one upper story window, is repeated on the gable end which faces Penobscot Bay.

Standing to the northwest of the house is a frame boathouse sheathed in board-and-batten siding. Farther to the north is a small brick building said to have been used to store flammable materials such as oil and kerosene. At present, an automated light, detached from the original building, functions as a navigational aid.

Historical Significance:

Located at the entrance to Gilkey's Harbor and the Village of Islesboro, Grindle Point Light Station has, for more than one-hundred years, been the pre-eminent landmark on this island of about 500 year-round inhabitants. First established in 1850 and rebuilt in 1875, the lighthouse is one of only three similarly shaped structures which still survive along the coast of Maine.

The light station at Grindle Point was built at a time of increased commercial traffic in Gilkey's Harbor. In 1847, for example, Islesboro was first included on a steamboat line between it and the mainland. Settlement of Islesboro commenced in 1769, and by 1860 its population reached 1,276 persons, its highest recorded figure. During the late nineteenth and early twentieth centuries the island became a popular summer resort area witnessed by the construction of sprawling hotels and cottages.

On March 3, 1849, the United States Navy appropriated $3,500 to build a lighthouse at Islesboro. A three-acre tract of land was acquired from Francis Grindle for $105, hence the name Grindle Point Light. The twenty-eight foot high tower and first keeper's house, built of brick, were completed in the summer of 1850. Rufus Dunning was appointed keeper of the light on August 20, 1850. He was replaced by Francis Grindle on April 3, 1853.

The 1875 annual report of the Lighthouse Board stated that the Grindle Point Lighthouse was in such condition:

"that it was determined advisable to re-build instead of repairing it. A one-and-one-half story building for the keeper's dwelling and a square brick tower for the light was therefore erected; the walls of the original house torn down to near the surface of the ground and the roof lowered. The original building thus changed will be used as a covered way between the new dwelling and the tower and for the storage of provisions, fuel, oil, and supplies of various kinds."

An appropriation for the rebuilding was made was made on June 23, 1874. A Boston contractor, who is as yet unidentified, performed the work, and a machine shop in Portland refurbished the replacement lens.

Few changes were made to the light station after it was rebuilt in 1874-75. At some point the boathouse was moved back five feet from the water and the board-and-batten siding added. In 1887 a brick cistern was built into the covered passage, and in 1896 a 1,000 pound hand-struck bell was added to the site.

Initial plans to automate the light station were made in 1923, but objections by local residents stalled the move until 1934. A twenty-one foot tall steel tower was built that year to carry a flashing white light. The de-activated station was acquired in 1935 by the Town of Islesboro for use as a public park and to house the Islesboro, now Sailor's Memorial Museum.

Additional Information

Francis Grindle (sometimes spelled Grindel), lighthouse keeper from 1853 to 1856, was the only keeper in Maine to serve in a lighthouse named for him.

After the tower light was deactivated in 1934, the town of Isleboro petitioned the Coast Guard to have the tower re-illuminated. Subsequently, in 1987, a modern optic was placed in the tower, which flashes green every four seconds. The 1934 skeletal tower was removed.

Best Viewing

The light station is accessible to the public via a 20-minute *Maine State Ferry* from Lincolnville Beach.

https://www.maine.gov/mdot/ferry/islesboro/

Distant views are available from parking areas along US Route 1 near the ferry terminal, which is located at the end of McKay Road in Lincolnville.

The Sailors Memorial Museum is located in the keeper's house and is open during the summer months. Check the following link for more information:

http://townofislesboro.com/departments/grindle-point-sailors-museum/

Grindle Point Light is also open to visitors one day per year on Maine Open Lighthouse Day. More information about this event can be found at:

http://www.lighthousefoundation.org/maine-open-lighthouse-day

36 Fort Point Light

Year Established: 1836
Nearest to: Stockton Springs
Latitude: 44° 28' 01" N
Longitude: 68° 48' 42" W
Tower Height: 31ft
Elevation: 88ft

Source: National Historic Register

Design: Square Tower
Designer(s): Unknown (1836)
Designer(s): U.S. Army Corps of Engineers (1857)
Material: Brick
Light Sequence: White light – Continuous
Fog Horn: One blast every 10 seconds

National Register of Historic Places (12/07/1987)

Physical Appearance:

The Fort Point Light Station consists of a square brick tower attached to a one-and-a-half -story L-shaped frame keeper's house. This structure is a replacement of the original light established in 1836. Surviving ancillary buildings include a brick oil house, a barn, and a bell house.

Fort Point's light tower, erected in 1857, rises to a height of twenty-six feet from its base to the center of the lantern. The square configuration is typical of other towers of this type built in Maine during the 1850s. It is capped by a square parapet which projects beyond the walls, and its original octagonal tower is surmounted by a spherical ventilator. There are two stairwell windows in the tower's south elevation. A narrow brick workroom links the tower to the dwelling.

The keeper's house, which also dates to 1857, has a three-bay west facade featuring a pair of six-over-six double-hung sash windows and a door sheltered by a small vestibule at the southwest corner. A long shed roofed dormer with two windows carries across the roof plane. This particular dormer was constructed over a pair of gable roofed dormers which were 1899 additions to the house. A brick flue punctuates the roof ridge. There are four windows in the north gable end and a door in the one story ell. The house is covered in clapboards, a replacement sheathing scheme from the original board-and-batten siding.

Historical Significance:

Established in 1836 at the entrance to the Penobscot River, the Fort Point Light Station has played a significant role in guiding shipping traffic to the important river ports of Bucksport and Bangor.

The Fort Point Light was constructed at a time of rapidly increasing maritime shipping on the Penobscot. Bucksport, the first important community upriver from the station, was a center of local commerce lumber production, and ship building. Some distance to the north of Bucksport, the city of Bangor built of its nineteenth century fortune on lumbering. Bangor underwent a phenomenal period of growth during the second quarter of the nineteenth century as a result of its strategic location with access to the interior lumber resources and the availability of a deep river anchorage. For decades this commercial traffic passed down the Penobscot River and in sight of the Fort Point Light.

Additional Information

Fort Point Light is on the original site of Fort Pownall, a British fortification located at the tip of Cape Jellison on the west side of the mouth of the Penobscot River, nearest to the town of Stockton Springs. Fort Point

Light is rare in its design, with a square tower on the exterior and a round brick lining on the interior.

The 31-foot square brick lighthouse, wood-frame two-story keeper's house, bell tower, barn, and oil house are all still standing, making Fort Point Light an unusually well-preserved light station, and one of the few that still has all of its structures from the 1800s.

Historically, vessels traveling north would anchor just beyond the light and await steam tugs that would tow them up the Penobscot River in order to load lumber in Bangor.

In 1988, Fort Point Light was automated, along with the West Quoddy Head Light – making Owls Head Light the last remaining manned lighthouse in Maine.

Under the Maine Lights Program coordinated by the Island Institute of Rockland, the lighthouse became the property of the State of Maine Bureau of Parks & Land in 1998. The lighthouse grounds are part of Fort Point State Park, a 120 acre park which also includes the remains of Fort Pownall.

Best Viewing

The lighthouse grounds are accessible to the public from and there is parking available. To reach the park, travel to the end of Lighthouse Road in Stockton Springs. The keeper's house is occupied by a Maine Park Ranger and his family. According to the park brochure, guided tours are available upon request:

"Fort Point State Park is open from 9:00am to sunset, Memorial Day through Labor Day. A fee is charged. If you would like to ask questions, make comments, or make reservations for guided tours, please contact us at the park office. Telephone: 207-941-4014"

Fort Point Light is also open to visitors one day per year on Maine Open Lighthouse Day. More information about this event can be found at:

http://www.lighthousefoundation.org/maine-open-lighthouse-day

37 Dice Head Light

Year Established: 1829
Nearest to: Castine
Latitude: 44° 22' 57" N
Longitude: 68° 49' 07" W
Tower Height: 51ft
Elevation: 134ft
Design: Conical Tower
1st Designer(s): Unknown (1829)
Material: Granite Rubble
Light Sequence: White light – 6 sec. on – repeating
Fog Horn: No fog signal

Source: U.S. Coast Guard

Lighthouse Appearance and History

Dice Head Light is one of only ten Maine lighthouses which are not registered with the National Register of Historic Places.

The light is located near the mouth of Penobscot River, nearest to the town of Castine. Castine is named for a French officer, Jean-Vincent d'Abbadie de Saint-Castin, who obtained a large land grant (circa 1654) in the area from King Louis XIV. During this time, northern Maine was part of Acadia and under French domain.

Castine is considered by some to be the oldest permanent settlement in New England, predating the Plymouth Colony by seven years

The light station is on land once owned by a family named Dyce. Although both spellings have often been used, the "Dice" spelling has endured.

The original conical granite rubble tower—42 feet tall from its base to the focal plane—and an adjacent one-and-one-half-story rubblestone dwelling were built in 1828, and a newspaper notice on November 5, 1828, announced that the light would go into service that evening.

In an 1843 report to Congress, it was stated that the light was useful for navigation to the harbor of Castine, but it was out of place to be of much help for the general navigation of Penobscot Bay and the Penobscot River entrance.

The Lighthouse Board considered discontinuing the light around 1857, but instead major repairs were carried out in 1858. The entire tower was surrounded with a six-sided wooden sheath (removed by 1907.) A fourth-order Fresnel lens replaced the original lamps and reflectors.

The light was electrified in 1935. Two years later the navigational light was moved to a skeleton tower closer to the shore. The keeper's house and surrounding land became the property of the Town of Castine a short time later. Then, in 1956, the lighthouse tower was turned over to the town.

By 1997, the granite tower began to lose more chunks of mortar, to the extent that inspectors found interior disintegration in the lighthouse that could eventually cause serious problems. A method of repair called "slurry injection" had to be employed. This process involved slurry—clay or cement mixed with a liquid—being injected through holes in the tower.

As a result, the voters of Castine approved spending $98,000 to repair the lighthouse. Another $25,000 was approved in March 1998. The town also received $52,000 from the *Maine Historic Preservation Committee. Campbell Construction Group* carried out the renovation.

In September 2007, a wind storm or "microburst" toppled the skeletal tower. In late October, at the request of the town, it was announced that the Coast Guard would install a new optic in the lighthouse tower, making it an active aid to navigation for the first time since 1937. A 250 mm optic went into service on January 1, 2008, exhibiting a white flash every 6 seconds.

Best Viewing

Dice Head Light is a short distance from the *Maine Maritime Academy* and is easily reached by driving to Castine on Route 166 and turning right on Battle Avenue. The grounds are open to the public daily until sunset. A path leads around the tower, affording good views.

Dice Head Light is open to visitors one day per year on Maine Open Lighthouse Day. More information about this event can be found at:

http://www.lighthousefoundation.org/maine-open-lighthouse-day

***

38 Pumpkin Island Light

Year Established: 1839
Nearest to: Deere Isle
Latitude: 44° 18' 33" N
Longitude: 68° 44' 34" W
Tower Height: 28ft
Elevation: 43ft

Source: National Archives

Design: Cylindrical Tower
Designer(s): U.S. Army Corps of Engineers (1839)
Material: Brick
Light Sequence: No light signal
Fog Horn: No fog signal

National Register of Historic Places (12/21/1987)

Physical Appearance:

Standing on a small island off the northwestern edge of Little Deer Isle, the Pumpkin Island Light Station consists of a cylindrical brick tower connected to a one-and-a-half-story frame keeper's house, both of which were built in 1854. A frame boathouse and brick oil house stand to the northeast.

The light tower is a relatively wide and squat structure which is twenty-two feet in height from its base to the middle of the lantern. A pair of windows are located in the northeastern face of the tower and an iron walkway and railing cap the brick shaft. The existing octagonal lantern, which is similar to others on late nineteenth century towers, replaced a larger ten or twelve sided unit. This was done in 1890. A narrow workroom with a door on the southeast side and an opposing window link the tower to the house.

Covered in clapboards, the dwelling has a three-bay facade featuring a side entrance and a pair of six-over-six double-hung sash windows. A dormer added in 1902 surmounts the center window on the facade and there are two at the rear. A bay window has been added to the southwest gable end of the house in front of the recessed one-story frame wing. This 1887 wing is punctuated by a number of door and window openings and has a small shed addition to its gable end. The rear elevation of the main block contains four windows and that of the wing has three. A chimney punctuates the roof of the house and a flue is located in the wing. When built in 1854, the keeper's house, like all of its contemporaries, was sheathed in board-and-batten siding. This material had probably been replaced by the 1880s.

Historical Significance:

Pumpkin Island Light Station, which was established in 1854, was constructed as a guide to the western entrance of Eggemoggin Reach, a narrow body of water that separates Little Dear Isle from the mainland.

The light station on Pumpkin Island was an integral component of a six unit system of primary navigational aids in East Penobscot Bay. All but two of these stations were built during the 1850s and after the organization of the Lighthouse Board when a complete system of aids was being developed. Located at the western end of Eggemoggin Reach, the Pumpkin Island light provided a guide to this heavily trafficked waterway linking Blue Hill Bay to the east and Penobscot Bay to the west.

A dry ledge beacon replaced the station in 1934, and the property was sold to a private citizen.

Additional Information

During the 19th century, there was a great need for lighthouses throughout the Penobscot Bay due to the demands of the lumber industry. Built on the western edge of the bay across from Grindle Point Light (built 15 years later,) Pumpkin Island Light was built to mark Eggemoggin Reach, where the Lighthouse Board noted it was "nearly as useful to commerce, and would be more so were there guides for entering it at night."

In 1934, Pumpkin head Light, along with 11 other lighthouses in Maine, was deactivated by the Coast Guard. The light station was replaced by a lighted buoy and sold to a Bar Harbor resident, who also purchased Winter Harbor Lighthouse and Massachusetts' Bird Island Lighthouse, all auctioned at the same time.

Pumpkin Island Light has been sold multiple times over the years and today remains in private hands.

Best Viewing

Pumpkin Island Light is visible from Eggemogan Road in the town of Deere Isle. The lighthouse and grounds are not open to the public.

***

39 Eagle Island Light

Year Established: 1839
Nearest to: Deer Isle
Latitude: 44° 13' 03" N
Longitude: 68° 46' 03" W
Tower Height: 30ft
Elevation: 106ft

Source: U.S. Coast Guard

Design: Conical Tower
Designer(s): Mr. Hildreth (1839)
Material: Rubblestone
Light Sequence: White light – 4 sec. on – repeating
Fog Horn: No fog signal

Lighthouse Appearance and History

Eagle Island Light is one of only ten Maine lighthouses which are not registered with the National Register of Historic Places.

Eagle Island is located in an area where Isle au Haut Bay meets East Penobscot Bay. The island is a 260 acre landmass, 1½ miles west of Deer Isle. Interestingly, there are seven other islands off the coast of Maine named Eagle Island.

The station consists of a rubblestone keepers dwelling along with a 30-foot-tall conical rubblestone lighthouse tower.

Conditions were primitive for keepers at Eagle Island Lighthouse. A two mile row was necessary to reach Deer Isle for supplies. On the return trip, the supplies had to be hauled up a steep and narrow trail to the bluff where the station was located. If the wind was blowing in the wrong direction, the boat had to be landed on the opposite end of the island, requiring an longer and more difficult trek with the supplies.

In spite of this, Eagle Island Light was considered to be a desirable assignment for light keepers. The station was home to plentiful of natural wildlife and was part of a friendly island community during the summer.

In the early 1960s, as Maine lighthouses become automated, the Coast Guard put all of the Eagle Island buildings, except the tower itself, up for auction under the condition that the buyer would remove the ancillary buildings from the light station property. Nobody was willing to try this virtually impossible feat, so in 1963 the Coast Guard chose to raze all the buildings except the tower. For unknown reasons, the empty bell tower was also left standing.

When the crew tried to remove the giant 4,200-pound fog bell, they lost control of it and it careened down the cliff into the ocean. A local lobsterman later found the bell and towed it to Great Spruce Head Island, where it was put on display and remains today.

Under the Maine Lights Program, ownership of the lighthouse was transferred in 1998 to a nonprofit group, the *Eagle Light Caretakers*.

Although the lighthouse is considered to be off-limits to the public, there appear to be events that open the tower. From a local newspaper:

(Originally published in Island Ad-Vantages, Aug 16, 2018)

Eagle Island Light gets a Facelift

"The nonprofit group the Eagle Light Caretakers hosted their annual open house Saturday, August 11, on Eagle Island, off the west side of Deer Isle. More than 50 people attended the event, which included tours of the light that recently underwent a "phase one" of renovations. Bob Quinn was the featured speaker, sharing stories about the light. Both Quinn

and his wife, Helene, are related to lightkeepers who tended the light. The light was commissioned in 1837 and was manned until 1959 when it was automated, according to a press release.

Renovations to date have included resetting lantern house windows, eliminating moisture ingress around the tower door, and repainting the structure. The work was completed by J.B. Leslie of Portsmouth, N.H., a company that has 12 Maine lighthouse projects to its credit.

The Eagle Light Caretakers anticipate a second round of work this fall that will focus on restoring the inside metal and wood of the lantern house."

For more information on Eagle Island Light open houses, refer to the calendar page posted by the Deer Isle Yacht Club: *http://www.deerisleyachtclub.com/*

Best Viewing

Eagle Island Light is visible at a distance from the end of Dunham Point Road in Deer Isle.

For a closer view, excursions are offered via the mail boat *Katherine* located in Sunset, Maine. The boat passes the Eagle Island Lighthouse while delivering mail to several other islands in the area. The ride runs approximately two hours. For more details:

https://www.eagleislandrentals.com/transportation

***

40 Goose Rocks Light

Year Established: 1890
Nearest to: North Haven
Latitude: 44° 08' 07" N
Longitude: 68° 49' 50" W
Tower Height: 51ft
Elevation: 51ft
Design: Spark Plug

Source: U.S. Coast Guard

Designer(s): U.S. Army Corps of Engineers (1890)
Material: Cast Iron
Light Sequence: Red or white light, depending on heading – 6 sec. on – repeating
Fog Horn: One blast every 10 seconds

National Register of Historic Places (12/07/1987)

Physical Appearance:

One of four so-called "spark plug" lights built in Maine, the Goose Rocks Light Station is a four-stage tapered cylindrical structure which stands on a shallow rock outcropping. The iron tower contains the keeper's quarters within its second stage and was originally equipped with a bell and boat launch.

The tower is composed of a concrete base sheathed in cast iron plates. This first stage is surmounted by an overhanging gallery supported by curvilinear brackets. It was originally sheltered by a roof that has since been removed. The gallery formed by these two components featured a plain tubular railing with vertical support posts and it sheltered windows and the entryway to the tapered second stage.

A three-floor division on the interior comprises the keeper's quarters. Three windows are positioned at equidistant points from each other on the second level and a trio of small bulls-eye windows occupies the third level. The latter are located immediately below the bracketed walkway that surrounds the tower's short third stage.

A door opens onto this walkway providing access to the short ladder and the crowning lantern stage. The octagonal lantern and its spherical ventilator are framed by another narrow walkway with railing. A solar panel has been added to the gallery since the station's automation.

Historical Significance:

Constructed in 1890, the Goose Rocks Light Station marks the east entrance to the Fox Island Thorofare between Vinalhaven and North Haven Islands. It stands on a shallow rock ledge and contains within its walls the keeper's quarters and storage facilities.

Goose Rocks Light occupies an important position in this heavily traveled thorofare. At the time of the light's construction Vinalhaven supported an important granite industry with two competitive firms, Bodwell Granite Company and the J.H. Sanborn Company. Both islands also attracted summer tourists, and a number of hotels and cottages were erected to serve the growing resort communities. The station was automated in 1963.

Additional Information

Goose Rocks is a ledge located between Stimpson Island (part of North Haven) and Widows Island (part of Vinalhaven.) The light station was established in 1890, at a time when Vinalhaven was the site of major granite quarries, and both communities were attracting a significant number of summer visitors.

To construct the lighthouse, a 24 foot cylindrical iron caisson, 25 feet in diameter, was anchored atop the ledge and sunk. The lower portion of the caisson was then filled with concrete, anchoring the caisson to the ledge below. Once the caisson was in place, work on the iron superstructure could begin.

When the light was declared surplus in the 1990s, a proposal was made to turn the building over to the town of North Haven, but this never materialized.

In 2006 the light was sold at auction to the non-profit *Beacon Preservation Inc.* of Connecticut: *"a nonprofit organization dedicated to the preservation of lighthouses and their environments for educational, cultural, recreational, and historical preservation purposes."*

Beacon Preservation offers overnight stays at the lighthouse, which it claims is the only offshore lighthouse on the eastern seaboard that offers accommodations: *http://www.beaconpreservation.org*

According to information from the above website, the Goose Rocks structure consists of a basement, four living levels, and a beacon tower:

- The ground level "Keep" is a cellar-style 22 foot diameter room with storage alcoves, dining table, cooking stove and kitchen area, and bathroom facilities.
- The 1st level "Sitting Room" is 18 feet in diameter, and offers seating for 8, a parlor stove, writing desk, and bookcase.
- The 2nd level "Keeper's Quarters" is 18 feet in diameter, and features a bed with nightstands, linen chest, writing desk, armoire, and reading chair.

- The 3rd level "Captain's Quarters" also 18 feet in diameter. It contains a bed, dresser, writing desk, and glass paneled cabinet.
- The 4th level "Crow's Nest" is 10 feet in diameter and consists of a set of bunk beds and a ladder leading up through a small hatch to the lantern.
- The "Beacon Room" is six feet in diameter, and houses the flashing light mechanism. The upper walls of the hexagon room are composed of red-tinted glass. A small hatch on the lower half of one wall leads to the exterior beacon deck.

Best Viewing

Goose Rocks Light is not visible from mainland points and can only be seen distantly from the surrounding island towns of Vinalhaven and North Haven.

The best viewing options are aboard cruises offered in the area, such as by Old Quarry Ocean Adventures of Stonington: *https://www.oldquarry.com/*

According to their website, Beacon Preservation features several "Lighthouse Day" open house events during the summer that allow the public to visit and walk through Goose Rocks Light at no cost.

Unfortunately, the calendar on this website does not indicate when these public viewing dates might occur. If you are interested in visiting Goose Rocks Light, it is suggested that you contact Beacon Preservation Inc. using the above link for more information.

41 Browns Head Light

Year Established: 1832
Nearest to: Vinalhaven
Latitude: 44° 06' 42" N
Longitude: 68° 54' 34" W
Tower Height: 18ft
Elevation: 39ft
Design: Cylindrical Tower
1st Designer(s): Jeremiah Berry (1832)
2nd Designer(s): Unknown (1855)
Material: Brick
Light Sequence: Red or white light, depending on heading – continuous
Fog Horn: One blast every 10 seconds

Source: National Archives

National Register of Historic Places (06/07/1982)

Physical Appearance:

Browns Head Light Station, dating from 1832, is a well preserved lighthouse with attached keeper's quarters located in a spectacular setting. The lighthouse proper is a cylindrical granite [sic] tower, approximately 18 feet in height, with a hexagonal light casing above topped by a hexagonal flat hipped cap. The light is 37 feet above the water and has a range of 15 miles.

The tower is connected to the keeper's house on the northeast side by a short covered passageway which enters the gable end of this Cape Cod structure.

The house is a story-and-a-half frame building, three bays wide on the long sides and two on the ends, The entrance is on the southeast side in the center. A one and a half story addition was added to the northeast end of the structure in 1927.

Historical Significance:

The light tower at Browns Head is one of the earliest designs, having been built during the year 1832 on order from President Andrew Jackson. It is the type of station in common use in the days before the Civil War. There was much shipping on Penobscot Bay when the light was erected and it became a key navigational aid particularly as a guide to the entrance of the much used Fox Islands Thoroughfare.

The keeper's house dates from 1857 when the station was rehabilitated-but the tower is original [sic]. This lighthouse has long been a mecca for summer visitors sailing their small boats on the Bay and Thoroughfare.

Additional Information

In 1855, the original 1832 rubblestone light tower at Browns Head was replaced by a cylindrical brick tower.

Brown's Head Light was automated in 1987, one of the last lighthouses in Maine to be automated. At the time of its automation, only Fort Point, West Quoddy Head, and Owls Head were still manually operated.

Under the Maine Lights Program, established by congressional legislation in 1996, the lighthouse buildings were transferred to the Town of Vinalhaven in 1998.

For many years, Brown's Head Light was the residence of Vinalhaven's town manager. On October 23, 2015, Browns Head Lighthouse was transferred from the Town of Vinalhaven to the *American Lighthouse Foundation*.

Best Viewing

Browns Head Light is located on Vinalhaven Island in Penobscot Bay, nearest the town of Vinalhaven. The light is not visible from mainland, but can be visited by taking the Vinalhaven ferry out of Rockland:

https://www.maine.gov/mdot/ferry/vinalhaven/

If taking the ferry to Vinalhaven from Rockland, it is best to bring your car to the island, as the lighthouse is several miles from the ferry landing.

***

42 Heron Neck Light

Year Established: 1854
Nearest to: Vinalhaven
Latitude: 44° 01' 30" N
Longitude: 68° 51' 43" W
Tower Height: 30ft
Elevation: 92ft

Source: National Historic Register

Design: Conical Tower
Designer(s): U.S. Army Corps of Engineers (1854)
Material: Brick
Light Sequence: Red or white light, depending on heading – continuous
Fog Horn: One blast every 30 seconds

National Register of Historic Places (12/07/1987)

Physical Appearance:

The Heron Neck Light Station is situated on a bold rock ledge which falls abruptly to the ocean. A station which has undergone numerous changes since it was first constructed in 1853, the present complex consists of a round brick tower connected to a one-and-a-half-story frame keeper's house and an oil house. A detached modern concrete block structure houses the fog horn.

The light tower, erected in 1853, is situated at the head of the range of buildings. Its brick shaft is punctuated on the seaward side by a pair of small stair windows. A wide iron parapet with a railing caps and projects over the tower shaft.

The polygonal lantern, which houses a modern beacon, is crowned by an iron roof and ventilator. It is an 1890 replacement of an earlier lantern. A documentary photograph of the tower reveals that it had a narrow parapet around a short brick shaft that supported the original lantern.

A narrow enclosed passageway with a small window on its east side links the tower to the dwelling. This L-shaped frame house was built in 1895-96 to replace the original brick dwelling. It is sheathed in clapboards and wood shingles and has a single window opening (now boarded shut) and two dormers on its south tower elevation. Its west gable end is punctuated by one window on each story. The broader east elevation features a pair of windows on both stories and a clipped gable roof. A small shed roofed porch shelters the door which opens into the narrow ell. There are two windows on the ell's gable end. Two brick flues punctuate the roof. The house rests on a granite foundation.

Historical Significance:

Heron Neck Light Station was established in 1853 as a guide to Carvers Harbor and Hurricane Sound. It is a component in the system of navigational aids in Penobscot Bay.

One of the principal communities served by the Heron Neck Light was Vinalhaven located at the north end of Carvers Harbor. Incorporated in 1789, Vinalhaven's population in 1850 was 1,252 persons, most of whom probably combined fishing with limited farming. Later in the century, Vinalhaven witnessed the development of a local granite quarry and tourist industry. The Heron Neck Light was also sited at the southeast entrance to Hurricane Sound, a body of water framing the west side of Vinalhaven Island and punctuated with islets.

The Complete Guide to Maine's Lighthouses

Additional Information

Heron Neck Lighthouse was constructed on the Heron Neck portion of Green Island to help guide mariners in Penobscot Bay in and out of the confines of Carver's Harbor on Vinalhaven Island.

Before the lighthouse was automated, one lighthouse keeper trained his Newfoundland dog *Nemo* to bark in response to ship whistles on foggy nights. Captains reported that Nemo's bark was louder than the fog signals in the bay.

The light was automated in 1982, and the Coast Guard keepers were removed. A new 300mm lens replaced the old Fresnel lens. In April 1989, an electrical fire broke out in the empty keeper's house. The house was badly damaged. Lacking funds to restore the dwelling, the Coast Guard proposed demolishing the structure. Strong public opposition to that plan sparked a discussion of alternative solutions.

The *Island Institute* of Rockland participated in this process and soon stepped in and offered to assume title to the lighthouse, auxiliary buildings, and the surrounding ten acres in exchange for restoring and maintaining the keeper's dwelling.

In November 1993 the Coast Guard agreed to hand over the lighthouse station to the Institute. The institute in turn leased the property to a Boston real estate developer who successfully restored the house.

In a somewhat controversial move, the individuals responsible for restoring the Heron Neck Light were granted full ownership in 2009 and public access was terminated.

Nonetheless, it was the Heron Neck project that inspired the Island Institute to initiate the Maine Lights Program, under which dozens of Maine lighthouses were turned over to local communities and nonprofit organizations.

Best Viewing

This light is located on Greens Island near the entrance to Hurricane Sound, nearest to the town of Vinalhaven. The light is not visible from any mainland location. This lighthouse is privately owned and not accessible to the public but can be viewed via boat tour in the area.

Matinicus Excursions offers a lighthouse cruise that passes by the Heron Neck Light. *Old Quarry Ocean Adventures* also provides views of the Heron Neck Light and five other lighthouses on its cruises. For more information, refer to the links below:

http://www.matinicusexcursions.com/

https://www.oldquarry.com/

43 Saddleback Ledge Light

Year Established: 1839
Nearest to: Vinalhaven
Latitude: 44° 00' 51" N
Longitude: 68° 43' 35" W
Tower Height: 36ft
Elevation: 52ft

Source: U.S. Coast Guard

Design: Conical Tower
Designer(s): Alexander Parris, Gridley Bryant (1839)
Material: Granite Block
Light Sequence: White light – 6 sec. on – repeating
Fog Horn: One blast every 10 seconds

National Register of Historic Places (01/29/1988)

Physical Appearance:

Standing resolutely on a bold rock outcropping, the Saddleback Ledge Light Station consists only of a conical granite tower. This structure dates to 1839 when the station was established. It was connected to a one-story rectangular frame building whose basement served as a boathouse. This building was a later addition to the complex although the date of construction has not been ascertained. The tower itself contains the keeper's quarters, kitchen and water cistern. The broad base of the tower quickly tapers to a projecting granite cap that supports the iron walkway and railing. Vertical rows of three small openings punctuate the tower's east and west faces, A door and one window are located in the north side. The ten sided lantern is covered by a polygonal roof and spherical ventilator. The center of the lantern is located thirty-six feet above the base of the structure. Both the lantern and deck were put here in 1883 in replacement of the original features. Documentary photographs show that the station also had a landing derrick and a pyramidal bell house elevated above the rock on a skeletal tower.

Historical Significance:

Established in 1839 on a precarious rock outcropping, Saddleback Ledge Light Station marks an eastward approach to Penobscot Bay.

Saddleback Ledge light was the second such complex built to guide maritime traffic into and out of Penobscot Bay. Eventually it was one of six principal navigational aids built along this important waterway. However, it was the only one of these six to have been classified as a secondary sea-coast light. The station was automated in 1954.

The tower at Saddleback Ledge was designed by Alexander Parris (1780-1852) and is similar in its overall form to the tower he designed two years earlier at Mount Desert Light Station. Saddleback clearly shows a proficiency in the use of granite as a material for construction, a characteristic for which the architect was well known. It is one of five known extant Parris designed towers or keeper's dwellings in Maine. A sixth, the tower at Whitehead Light Station, is also attributed to him.

Additional Information

Saddleback Ledge s a ¼-acre granite outcropping at the southern entrance to East Penobscot Bay (also known as Isle au Haut Bay), approximately four miles from the southeastern corner of Vinalhaven to the west and three miles from the southwestern coast of Isle au Haut to the east.

Saddleback Ledge Light has been described as one of the most remote and barren of all Maine lighthouse locations.

Offshore lighthouses like Saddleback Ledge were always the last to receive indoor plumbing, electricity, and telephones. Foul weather would isolate keepers and their families for weeks at a time.

Like Boon Island and Mount Desert Rock, Saddleback Ledge has absolutely no soil. As they did at those other remote stations, the keepers at Saddleback Ledge brought soil from the mainland each spring and planted a few vegetables and flowers. The soil would inevitably be swept away by winter storms.

Alexander Parris wrote that he had personally overseen the construction on Saddleback Ledge Light. The granite block construction was carried out by Gridley J.F. Bryant, who worked with Parris on several buildings in the 1840s.

Because the ledge was known to be one of the toughest locations to land a boat, in 1885, a derrick with a swinging arm and attached chair was added to help in getting keepers and visitors on and off the tricky rock ledge.

As with the Two Bush Island Light, in 1960 the Coast Guard allowed the 10th Special Forces Group from Massachusetts to blow up the Saddleback Ledge keeper's dwelling in a training exercise. Today, only the light tower remains.

In 2009, the light tower was deemed excess by the Coast Guard, and was offered at no cost to eligible entities, including federal, state, and local agencies, non-profit corporations, and educational organizations under the provisions of the National Historic Lighthouse Preservation Act.

Unfortunately, with its remote, inhospitable location, no group or individual offered take the light on as a preservation project. To this day, Saddleback Ledge Light is the only Maine lighthouse that is still owned and operated solely by the Coast Guard.

Best Viewing

Saddleback Ledge Light is located in southern Penobscot Bay in the Isle Au Haut bay, nearest to the town of Vinalhaven. This lighthouse is not open to the public nor is a visible from mainland locations. It is best viewed by boat cruises offered in the area.

As with Heron Neck Light, *Matinicus Excursions* offers a lighthouse cruise that passes by the Saddleback Ledge Light. *Old Quarry Ocean Adventures* also provides views of the light and five other lighthouses on its cruises. For more information, refer to the links below:

http://www.matinicusexcursions.com/

https://www.oldquarry.com/

44 Isle au Haut Light (Robinson Point Light)

Year Established: 1907
Nearest to: Isle au Haut
Latitude: 44° 03' 53" N
Longitude: 68° 39' 04" W
Tower Height: 40ft
Elevation: 48ft
Design: Cylindrical Base/Conical Tower
Designer(s): U.S. Army Corps of Engineers (1907)
Material: Granite Block Base/Brick Tower
Light Sequence: Red or white light, depending on heading – 4 sec. on – repeating
Fog Horn: No fog signal

Source: National Archives

National Register of Historic Places (12/07/1987)

Physical Appearance:

The Isle Au Haut Light Station consists of a detached granite and brick light tower reached by way of an elevated wooden walkway and a two-story gambrel roofed, stucco keeper's dwelling, a stucco oil house, a frame boathouse, a fuel house, and a privy. The tower rises above a wide rock ledge whereas the house and ancillary buildings stand on the shore framed by evergreens.

Isle Au Haut's tower, built in 1907, is composed of a conical granite base, twenty four feet in height, that supports a cylindrical brick shaft which is sixteen feet tall. The brick shaft is punctuated by a door on the southeast face and two fifteen pane windows on the northeast and southwest sides. A wide overhanging parapet with a railing caps the tower. Behind it is an octagonal lantern with a polygonal roof and spherical ventilator. A long elevated walkway links the base of the brick shaft to the shore.

Historical Significance:

The Isle Au Haut Light Station is the next to last complex of its type established in Maine. Built in 1907 on Robinson Point at the southern end of Isle Au Haut Thorofare, the light was established here as a guide to the adjacent sheltered harbor.

The 1902 edition of the Annual Report of Light-House Board carries a lengthy discussion about the need for a light at this site. Because of the rich fishing grounds along the lower East Penobscot Bay, the harbor at Isle Au Haut was found to be the most convenient harbor of refuge for fishing trawlers. Despite this clear statement of need, however, Congress did not authorize construction until June 23, 1906, when it appropriated $14,000 for the station. It was activated on December 30, 1907. In 1934 the light was automated and the buildings, with the exception of the tower, were sold. At present the dwelling houses a bed and breakfast inn.

Additional Information

Isle Haute fittingly translates to "high island," as the elevation of Isle au Haut reaches a high point 556 feet above sea level. Most houses in the town of Isle au Haut do not have electricity. Today there are about 50 year-round residents, with a higher population in the summer.

The Isle au Haut lighthouse is a brick tower on a granite base, very similar in construction to the lighthouses built earlier at Marshall Point (1857) and Ram Island (1888). These are the only three lighthouses in Maine that utilize a granite-block-and-brick design. Their similarity suggests that Major Charles Raymond of the Army Corps of Engineers may have been involved in the design of all three lights.

The light, now solar powered, continues to flash red with a white sector as an active aid to navigation maintained by the Coast Guard. Under the Maine Lights Program, the lighthouse was turned over to the Town of Isle au Haut in April 1998.

A complete restoration of the lighthouse tower was finished in June 1999. $62,000 was raised for the overhaul by concerned residents of the island, who formed *Friends of the Isle au Haut Lighthouse*:

> *https://www.isleauhautlighthouse.org/*

Best Viewing

This light is located on Robinson Point, on the west coast of Isle au Haut. The lighthouse grounds are open to the public.

The keeper's house operated as a bed and breakfast inn known as the *Keeper's House Inn* from 1986-2019. According to the link below, the keeper's house is currently for sale but currently available as a self-catered seasonal weekly rental.

> *http://keepershouse.com/*

Isle au Haut Light is not visible from the mainland but can be reached by taking the mail boat/passenger ferry out of Stonington.

> *http://isleauhautferryservice.com/*

A close up view of the light tower requires a hike of a little under a mile from the ferry landing.

***

45 Deer Island Thorofare Light (Mark Island Light)

Year Established: 1858
Nearest to: Deere Isle
Latitude: 44° 08' 03" N
Longitude: 68° 42' 11" W
Tower Height: 25ft
Elevation: 52ft
Design: Square Tower
Designer(s): Unknown (1858)
Material: Brick
Light Sequence: White light – 6 sec. on – repeating
Fog Horn: One blast every 15 seconds

Source: National Archives

Lighthouse Appearance and History

Deer Island Thorofare Light is one of only ten Maine lighthouses which are not registered with the National Register of Historic Places.

Perhaps the most confusing off all Maine lighthouse names, Deer Island Thorofare Light actually sits on six-acre Mark Island, two miles offshore from nearby Stonington. Mark Island is at the west end of the Deer Island Thorofare and of Merchant Row, two east-west ocean passages among a group small islands which lie between Deer Isle and Isle au Haut.

Curiously, the large island to the north of the light station and the town on it are "Deer Isle", but the sea passage is called "Deer Island Thorofare". To make things even worse, the island on which the lighthouse resides is called "Mark Island" on some NOAA charts, but "Marks Island" on other charts.

And in a final bit of irony, there are two different Maine light stations referred to as "Mark Island Light" by local residents – Deer Island Thorofare Light and Winter

Harbor Light which resides on – you guessed it – Mark Island in Winter Harbor.

Naming aside, the Deer Island Thorofare Light is a 25-foot-tall, square brick tower which was originally fitted with a fourth-order Fresnel lens showing a fixed white light 52 feet above mean high water, first lighted on New Year's Day in 1858. The light now consists of a modern LED optic.

The tower is attached to a 1½ story wood-frame keeper's dwelling. Similar in design to the Fort Point Light, the square tower is actually round on the inside, with a spiral stairway leading to the lantern room.

For many years, mail deliveries to Mark Island were rather complicated. A storekeeper in Rockland would give newspapers and the mail to the captain of some vessel heading east. When the vessel approached Mark Island, the bundle would be tossed into the water. The lighthouse keeper then would row out to retrieve the package.

On December 15, 1997, the Maine Lighthouse Selection Committee, formed to oversee the transfer of 35 Maine lighthouses under the Maine Lights Program, announced that Deer Island Thorofare Light would be turned over by the Coast Guard to the *Island Heritage Trust*: https://www.islandheritagetrust.org

This group maintains the island as a wildlife refuge for bald eagles and nesting eider ducks.

To commemorate the transfer of the light station, a book, *Mark Island Light,* was published by Heritage Trust member Marnie Reed Crowell. According to the Island Heritage Trust website, the book is a comprehensive history of the light, its keepers and operational details, including such information as a description of the lens and the horn, and includes vintage and contemporary photographs, drawings, and excerpts from journals, letters and newspapers. For information on purchasing this book, refer to the Island Heritage Trust link above.

Best Viewing

The Deer Island Thorofare Light grounds are not open to the public but can be seen distantly from Sand Beach Road in Stonington.

A much better view is available from area sightseeing cruises such the one offered by the Isle au Haut Company, also in Stonington:
http://isleauhautferryservice.com

***

46 Blue Hill Bay Light

Year Established: 1857
Nearest to: Brooklin
Latitude: 44° 14' 56" N
Longitude: 68° 29' 55 W
Tower Height: 22ft
Elevation: 21ft
Design: Cylindrical Tower
Designer(s): Unknown (1857)
Material: Brick
Light Sequence: No light signal
Fog Horn: No fog signal

Source: National Archives

Lighthouse Appearance and History

Blue Hill Bay Light is one of only ten Maine lighthouses which are not registered with the National Register of Historic Places.

Blue Hill Bay lies just west of Penobscot Bay. The two bays are connected by Eggemoggin Reach, a small channel of water across the landmass protruding from the mainland. Blue Hill Bay marks the eastern side of Mount Desert Island, and further north, Acadia National Park and Frenchman Bay.

The Blue Hill Bay Light station is located on Green Island, situated on the west side of the entrance to the bay for which the light station is named. The station has also been known as "Eggemoggin Lighthouse" and "Sand Island Light".

The 22 foot light tower was activated in 1857. The lighthouse is connected by a brick passageway to a wood-frame 1½ story keeper's house. A barn, boathouse, and outhouse were also built; an oil house was added in 1905.

In 1935, the light was removed from the brick tower and replaced by a skeleton structure.

A retired accountant from New Jersey purchased the lighthouse in 1976 for use as a private residence and added several improvements, including a long floating walkway and a deep water mooring, giving easy access to the island during all tides.

Since 1995, the lighthouse has been sold multiple times, and remains in private hands today.

Best Viewing

This light is located on Green Island in Blue Hill Bay, nearest to the town of Brooklin. Blue Hill Bay Light is not accessible to the public but may be viewed via boat tours in the area.

Blue Hill Light can be seen distantly from Neskeag Road in Brooklin. The best views of Blue Hill Bay Light are from the water. Bar Harbor Whale Watch Co. offers periodic cruises of many lighthouses in Penobscot and Blue Harbor Bays. For more information:

https://www.barharborwhales.com/

47 Burnt Coat Harbor Light

Year Established: 1872
Nearest to: Swans Island
Latitude: 44° 08' 02" N
Longitude: 68° 26' 49" W
Tower Height: 32ft
Elevation: 75ft
Design: Square Tower

Source: National Historic Register

Designer(s): U.S. Army Corps of Engineers (1872)
Material: Brick
Light Sequence: White light – 4 sec. on – repeating
Fog Horn: No fog signal

National Register of Historic Places (12/07/1987)

Physical Appearance:

The Burnt Coat Harbor Light Station, like a number of others built or rebuilt in the early 1870s, consists of a square tapered brick tower connected to an L-shaped keeper's house that is sheathed in clapboards. A bell house and oil house also survive.

The tower, which rises to a height of thirty-two feet from its base to the middle of the lantern, is capped by a square iron walkway with railing. It was built in 1872. A spherical ventilator crowns the ten-sided lantern. There are two twenty eight pane casement windows on the west face of the tower and a door at the base on the north elevation. The latter was formerly covered by a passageway which linked the tower to the house.

When first built, the station had a range light system employing a pair of widely spaced towers. The second light stood near the site of the present bell house and a covered passageway, built in 1881, connected the two structures. The front range light was discontinued in 1884 and subsequently removed.

Historical Significance:

The Burnt Coat Harbor Light Station was established in 1872 as a guide to Burnt Coat Harbor on Swan's Island.

The 1871 edition of the Annual Report of the Light-House Board states that the range light at Burnt Coat Harbor was erected as a guide to this harbor of refuge. It further commented that "this harbor is commodious and safe, and is a distant 36 miles from the nearest place of safe anchorage on that coast." The virtually intact exterior features of the dwelling and tower are important examples of the form which these components took in the early 1870s.

Additional Information

Burnt Coat Harbor Light is located on Swans Island, named after Colonel James Swan of Scotland, who purchased the island and surrounding land in 1786. Since the 1970s, the 81 square mile island has been home to approximately 300 full time residents.

The light station was originally designed as a set of two ranging lights, consisting of a small square tower in the front and the current larger tower in the rear. For more information on how range lights were utilized by mariners, refer to the description in Chapter 16 - *Doubling Point Range Light*.

Unfortunately, the range lights at Burnt Coat Harbor caused confusion with mariners, which led to shipwrecks. In response to this, the Lighthouse Board deactivated and dismantled the smaller front tower in 1884.

Burnt Coat Harbor's name origin is a source of debate. Some say it comes from a Revolutionary War soldier who burnt his coat as a sign of rebellion. Others say the source is Samuel de Champlain, who called the area "Brule-Cote," or Burnt Coast, presumably because it was populated with numerous campfires.

The light was automated by the Coast Guard 1975. At that time, the original fourth-order Fresnel lens was removed and replaced by an automatic light on a skeleton tower nearby. The new light wasn't as bright as the old one, and after numerous complaints the Coast Guard removed the skeletal tower and relighted the lighthouse with an automatic 250mm optic, which was again updated in 2017 to a modern LED optic.

In 1994, the entire light station was transferred to the town of Swans Island, and the group *Friends of Swans Island Lighthouse* was formed to preserve this historic landmark. Since then, extensive renovation has occurred.

A very informative website managed by the Friends of Swans Island Lighthouse can be found here:

https://www.burntcoatharborlight.com/

This website includes information about Swans Island as well as Burnt Coat Harbor Light history, renovation details, hours, and information regarding rentals at the keeper's house.

Best Viewing

The lighthouse grounds and light tower are open to the public during summer months. The island can be accessed via a 30 minute ferry from Bass Harbor. If traveling to Swans Island by ferry, it will be necessary to bring your vehicle or bicycle, as the Burnt Coat Harbor Light is four miles from the island ferry terminal.

https://www.maine.gov/mdot/ferry/swansisland/

Burnt Coat Harbor is regarded by some as one of the most beautiful harbors in Maine, with the lighthouse on Hockamock Head giving a very picturesque look to the area.

Burnt Coat Harbor Light is also open to visitors during Maine Open Lighthouse Day. More information about this event can be found at:

www.lighthousefoundation.org/maine-open-lighthouse-day

48 Bass Harbor Head Light

Year Established: 1858
Nearest to: Bass Harbor
Latitude: 44° 13' 18" N
Longitude: 68° 20' 14" W
Tower Height: 32ft
Elevation: 56ft

Source: National Archives

Design: Cylindrical Tower
Designer(s): U.S. Army Corps of Engineering (1858)
Material: Brick
Light Sequence: Red light – 4 sec. on – repeating
Fog Horn: No fog signal

National Register of Historic Places (12/07/1987)

Physical Appearance:

Standing on a bold rock ledge, Bass Harbor Head Light Station consists of a circular brick tower connected to a one-and-a-half-story frame keeper's quarters. Detached from the tower is a small rectangular bell house, an oil house and a barn.

The light tower, built in 1858, is twenty-six feet in height from its base to the original focal plane of the beacon. Its brick walls are punctuated by a pair of small windows facing Blue Hill Bay. Capped by a walkway and iron railing the tower supports a polygonal lantern whose iron base features paired round arched panels in each face. A modern beacon has replaced the original lens. A narrow frame, covered passage supported on a stone foundation links the tower with the house. Its south wall is punctuated by a single small window and the exterior walls, like those on the keeper's quarters and bell house, are covered in replacement vinyl siding.

The T-shaped house has a three-bay front (west) elevation featuring a narrow vestibule at the northwest corner and a shed roofed dormer centrally located on the roof. Like the tower it was constructed in 1858. The window openings retain their six-over-six double-hung sash. There are four windows, two on each story, on the gable ends. A brick flue punctuates the roof and a second dormer is located on the rear elevation. The one-story ell, which was lengthened by ten feet in 1900, extends from the east elevation. In 1878 the house was raised ten inches and the original board-and-batten siding replaced with clapboards. The clapboards have since been covered with vinyl siding.

The compound on which the light station stands is bordered by a low concrete retaining wall. This is apparently a modern feature since it does not appear in early twentieth century documentary photographs of the site.

Historical Significance:

The light station at Bass Harbor Head was established in 1858 during a period of increased effort by the Federal government to provide aids to navigation along the coast. Its location at this site was designed to aid vessels coming into Bass Harbor, a small fishing village located to the northwest of the light. The station was automated in 1974.

Additional Information

With an area of 108 square miles, Mount Desert Island is the largest island off the coast of Maine, and the second largest island on the eastern seaboard, after New York's Long Island. When Samuel de Champlain saw the island form the sea, he noted its summits were bare, and gave it the name "île des Monts Déserts," or island of the Bare Mountains.

Mount Desert Island is ringed by numerous smaller islands, six of which are marked by lighthouses:

- Blue Hill Bay Light
- Burnt Coal Harbor Light
- Egg Rock Light
- Great Duck Island Light
- Baker Island Light
- Bear Island Light

Bass Harbor Head is the only lighthouse on Mount Desert Island itself, situated at the island's southernmost point.

In 2012, Bass Harbor Head Lighthouse was featured on the back of a quarter issued as part of the U.S. Mint's "America the Beautiful Quarters Program." The lighthouse received more publicity in 2016 when the U.S. Postal Service issued a stamp featuring a photo of the lighthouse in observance of the National Park Service's 100th anniversary.

Source: U.S. Mint

Source: U.S. Postal Service

In September 2017, the Coast Guard offered to transfer ownership of Bass Harbor Head Lighthouse and two-and-a-half acres of land to the National Park Service to become park of Acadia National Park.

The Park Service did not take long to make a decision on assuming ownership of the lighthouse, as they announced in November 2017 that they would take possession of the property.

Best Viewing

This lighthouse is located at the southern tip of Mount Desert Island at the end of Lighthouse Road in Bass Harbor.

The lighthouse grounds are accessible to the public all year round with parking available. The lighthouse is a popular tourist spot and is considered one of the most photographed lighthouses in New England.

Bass Harbor Head Light is open to visitors one day per year on Maine Open Lighthouse Day. More information about this event can be found at:

http://www.lighthousefoundation.org/maine-open-lighthouse-day

49 Great Duck Island Light

Year Established: 1890
Nearest to: Frenchboro
Latitude: 44° 08' 31" N
Longitude: 68° 14' 44" W
Tower Height: 36ft
Elevation: 67ft

Source: National Archives

Design: Cylindrical Tower
Designer(s): U.s> Army Corps of Engineers (1890)
Material: Brick
Light Sequence: Red light – 5 sec. on – repeating
Fog Horn: One blast every 15 seconds

National Register of Historic Places (01/29/1988)

Physical Appearance:

Prominently situated at the southern end of Great Duck Island, this light station is composed of a circular brick tower with workroom, a detached keeper's house, fog signal building, oil house, and a small shed.

The light tower at Great Duck Island, constructed in 1890, is a cylindrical brick structure that rises to a height of thirty-five-and-a-half feet from its base to the center of the lantern. Punctuated by three small openings (now filled with glass blocks) the tower is capped by a handsome bracketed iron parapet with railing.

Centrally located behind the railing is the ten-sided lantern. The narrow brick workroom extends from the west face of the tower. It has an opening below the west gable end and a glass block window on the south side.

Standing at a considerable distance to the north of the tower is the keeper's house; the lone survivor of the three originally erected here in 1890. The one-and-a-half-story wooden frame dwelling has a narrow, centrally located shed roofed porch on its three-bay front (east) elevation and a shed at the rear. Gable roofed dormers are positioned on both the front and rear facades. A pair of brick flues punctuate the roof ridge. Clapboards cover the house. Paired windows are located in both gable ends.

At the time of its establishment the light station on Great Duck Island also featured, in addition to the two dwellings, a boathouse and slip 200 feet in length, a barn, a long rain shed used to collect water for the fog signal, an engine house, coal bunkers, and a number of small outbuildings. Most of these ancillary buildings had been removed prior to the automation of the light in 1986.

Historical Significance:

Great Duck Island Light Station was established in 1890 as a secondary seacoast light strategically located between the primary light on Mount Desert Rock and the approach to Blue Hill Bay and Mount Desert Island.

The construction of Great Duck Island Light Station illustrates the continued effort by the Light-House Board to establish an integral system of navigational aids along the coast of Maine. In its 1885 Annual Report the Board first recognized the need for a light at this location. Three years later the Annual Report pointed to the increased "...importance of Mount Desert and the vicinity as a summer resort", and further stated the need for a fog signal "...not only for the general coastwise commerce, but for the safety of the steamers and yachts frequenting Frenchman's Bay."

Additional Information

Great Duck Island is estimated to support an astounding twenty percent of Maine's entire seabird population. The 200-acre island's name was derived from the pond in its center that attracts large flocks of ducks each spring.

Because of its remote location and relatively high maintenance needs, three keepers' dwellings of six rooms each were built side by side near the lighthouse.

The large keeper's quarters were a blessing for assistant lighthouse keeper Adam Reed, who occupied the light station from 1902-1912 with his wife Emma and their sixteen children. They are believed to be the largest family in American lighthouse history. So large, in fact, that the Coast Guard agreed to utilize a barn at the station as a makeshift school for eighteen students — fourteen Reed children, two from another keeper, and two from the north end of the island.

In 1984, the Maine Chapter of the Nature Conservancy purchased most of Great Duck Island. After Great Duck Island Lighthouse was automated in 1986, the Coast Guard destroyed all but one of the keeper's houses, as well as most of the outbuildings.

In 1998, the roughly twelve acres encompassing Great Duck Island Lighthouse became the property of Bar Harbor's *College of the Atlantic* under the Maine Lights Program. The college also maintains a research facility at Mount Desert Rock Light. Today, Great Duck Island today serves as a biology, ecology, and wildlife study center. For more information:

https://www.coa.edu/islands/great-duck-island/

Best Viewing

Great Duck Island Light is located along the Blue Hill Bay approach to the island, nearest to the town of Frenchboro. The lighthouse is not visible from the mainland and is not accessible to the public.

Bar Harbor Whale Watch Co. offers periodic cruises of many lighthouses around Mount Desert Island, including Great Duck Island. For more information:

https://www.barharborwhales.com/

The Complete Guide to Maine's Lighthouses

50 Mount Desert Rock Light

Year Established: 1830
Nearest to: Frenchboro
Latitude: 43° 58' 07" N
Longitude: 68° 07' 42" W
Tower Height: 58ft
Elevation: 75ft
Design: Conical Tower
1st Designer(s): Joseph Berry (1830)
2nd Designer(s): Alexander Parris, Joseph W. Coburn (1847)
Material: Granite Block
Light Sequence: White light – 15 sec. on - repeating
Fog Horn: Two blasts every 30 seconds

Source: National Archives

National Register of Historic Places (3/14/1988)

Mount Desert Rock Light was listed in the National Register of Historic Places in 1988, but unfortunately the nomination form is marked as "missing" by the National Archives. In its place, with permission, are excerpts from the website http://www.lighthousefriends.com:

Congress allocated $5,000 in 1829 for a lighthouse "on the most eligible" spot on Mount Desert Rock. Gamaliel E. Smith made a low-ball bid, and by the time the lighthouse was to be completed in mid-October, his crewmen, who were forced to work without proper tools, had only excavated part of the cellar. Smith was accordingly dismissed, and Joseph Berry, another contractor who made a bid of $2,770 on the project and who had recently completed the lighthouse at Hendricks Head, was hired to complete the work. Berry finished the original Mount Desert Rock Lighthouse, consisting of a stone dwelling surmounted by a wooden tower and "bird cage" lantern, in the summer of 1830...

...The original 1830 optic consisted of a chandelier of ten Argand lamps backed by fourteen-inch reflectors displayed at a *focal plane of fifty-six feet above sea level. This was not good enough to be an effective aid to navigation, and in 1847 Congress authorized $15,000 for the "rebuilding" of the lighthouse on Mount Desert Rock. The new lighthouse, which was separate from the dwelling, was described in an 1850 report as "a beautiful tower, built of heavy granite stone, and just such a building as the locality needed, to stand the furry of the elements." The keeper and his family still lived in the old stone dwelling, as it was more "convenient for the family to do their work in," but it was felt that if a kitchen was built onto the lighthouse, it would be a "very suitable place" for their work, if the keeper decided to abandon the dwelling and move into the granite tower. In 1857, the newly formed Lighthouse Board supplied a new lantern room and third-order Fresnel lens for the tower...*

...In 1876, a one-and-a-half-story frame dwelling was built on the rock just south of the old stone dwelling that was still being used by the keepers. As the top of the lighthouse was leaky, making the structure uninhabitable, its stone parapet was removed in 1880, and a cast-iron lantern deck and gallery were installed. At this time, new window frames were put in and the exterior walls of the tower were repointed...

...Mount Desert Rock was a desolate place, with practically nothing growing there. Fishermen would show their thanks for the light by bringing grain bags of dirt to the rock each spring. The American Weekly reported in 1934 how the rock had developed a reputation of being a "floral paradise" for a few months each summer:

> *"The dirt the fishermen bring off is carefully packed in between the crevices and seeds of many varieties are sown and carefully tended. Strangely enough they nearly all thrive in the cold moist atmosphere. Visitors approaching the rock during the summer and early fall are amazed at*

the kaleidoscope of color that greets the eye on the barren ledge.

With the first fall frosts, the garden disappears, and long before the winter is over, the raging storms that literally throw huge waves across the rock area wash every vestige of soil from the offshore rock garden. Long before spring comes around again not even a spoonful of soil is left on the rock."

Additional Information

Mount Desert Rock Light is the most isolated lighthouse in the state of Maine, located offshore, some 25 nautical miles from Bar Harbor.

Not long after the lighthouse was automated in 1977, the *College of the Atlantic* received permission to use the island for whale research. The station was transferred to the college permanently in 1998 and continues its dual role as an active aid to navigation, as well as a whale research outpost. For more information on the research work: *https://www.coa.edu/islands/mount-desert-rock/*

In 2014, the Mars family, well-known for their sales of candy bars, donated $425,000 to upgrade the facilities at Mount Desert Rock.

As with other offshore light stations in Maine, Mount Desert Rock Light contains survival gear for use by any shipwrecked or lost mariners who may find themselves stranded on this isolated remote location.

Best Viewing

Mount Desert Rock Light is located approximately 20 miles south of Mount Desert Island nearest to the town of Frenchboro.

This lighthouse is not visible from the mainland, nor open to the public and not serviced by any regularly scheduled boat tours.

Whale watch cruises leaving from Bar Harbor occasionally pass Mount Desert Rock Light, but only when whales are spotted in the area.

51 Baker Island Light

Year Established: 1839
Nearest to: Isleboro
Latitude: 44° 14' 28" N
Longitude: 68° 11' 17" W
Tower Height: 43ft
Elevation: 105ft
Design: Cylindrical
1st Designer(s): Unknown (1839)
2nd Designer(s): U.S. Army Corps of Engineers (1855)
Material: Brick
Light Sequence: White light – 10 sec. on – repeating
Fog Horn: No fog signal

Source: National Historic Register

National Register of Historic Places (01/05/1988)

Physical Appearance:

The Baker Island Light Station is located on a small island which is now part of Acadia National Park, The complex, situated nearly seventy feet above sea level, consists of a cylindrical brick tower, a detached one-and-a-half story frame keeper's house, an oil house, and a fuel house.

Attaining a height of thirty-seven feet from its base to the lens focal plane, the tower, built in 1855, is entered from a door facing the house. Originally covered by a passageway, the door is flanked by the surviving square brick walls which are joined to the round tower. Two window openings, now covered, are located in the tower's south and north face respectively. They illuminate the interior spiral stair. An iron walkway with a railing projects slightly over the walls. An octagonal iron lantern with clear glass panes in its upper section surmounts the tower. It is capped by a domed polygonal roof featuring a spherical ventilator. The 1903 Annual

Report of the Light-House Board makes reference to a reinforcement of the tower, but the exact nature of this undertaking is not clear.

Constructed in 1855, the keeper's house is an L-shaped building sheathed in clapboards that rests on a brick foundation. Its three-bay facade has a door at the northeast corner and two window openings (now boarded over). Shallow pediments frame these openings. A gable roofed dormer surmounts the central window and a brick chimney punctuates the roof ridge. There are four symmetrically placed windows on the west gable end and three on the east end.

Originally, a door was located on this tower end. There are two windows on the rear elevation of the main block as well as a second dormer. The short ell has a window and narrow shed roofed vestibule on the east side, a single window at the rear and a door and one window on the wall, a brick flue rises through the ell.

A documentary photograph of the Baker Island Light Station shows that the existing tower and house have undergone a number of changes since they were built in 1855. The dwelling's clapboards replace the original board-and-batten siding and the dormers are later additions. Further alterations were made with the removal of the narrow connecting passageway between the house and tower.

Historical Significance:

Standing at the summit of Baker Island, the Baker Island Light Station is a relatively intact example of an 1850s Maine complex.

The light station at Baker Island was established in 1828 as a guide to the south entrance to Frenchman's Bay and Mount Desert Island, Its strategic location as a navigational aid is emphasized by the number of coastal communities in the vicinity as well as its role in guiding vessels along the coast between the lights at Saddleback Ledge to the southwest and Petit Manan to the northeast.

It was the first light station established in the vicinity of Mount Desert Island. During the late nineteenth century the Baker Island Light guided the numerous vessels which came to Mount Desert bearing tourists for the resorts at Bar Harbor, Northeast Harbor and others. The tower continues to serve as an aid to navigation under the supervision of the Coast Guard. The keeper's dwelling and ancillary buildings have been transferred to Acadia National Park as has the entire island.

Additional Information

Baker Island Light is located within the Cranberry Islands of Acadia National Park, nearest to the town of Isleboro. 123-acre Baker Island is the outermost of the five Cranberry Isles, the other four being: Great Cranberry, Little Cranberry, Sutton, and Bear.

Located at the entrance to Mount Desert Island's Southwest Harbor, the islands are named for the bright red berries found over much of them in the fall. Legend has it that in 1812, Baker Island was unclaimed and unoccupied, and a family "simply took possession of it."

The original 1839 tower was built of rubblestone, and stood twenty-six feet tall. It was topped by an octagonal lantern, with a wrought iron frame and copper dome. The lantern housed tens lamps, backed by fifteen-inch reflectors and arranged in two rows, one above the other.

In 1853, a report from the Lighthouse Board noted that the tower on Baker Island was "entirely worthless," and the keeper's dwelling was "so old and leaky" that it was unhealthy. Two years later, the dwelling and tower were rebuilt for $4,963 on the island's highest point of land, far from the sea, and a modern fourth-order Fresnel lens was installed in the lantern room.

In 1958, the keeper's dwelling was transferred to the National Park Service, leaving the Coast Guard with just the lighthouse tower. Several times during the 1990s, the Coast Guard stated its desire to discontinue the light, but feedback from local residents convinced them that the light should remain active.

The lighthouse tower was offered to non-profit and government groups in 2008 as part of the National Historic Lighthouse Preservation Act, and was awarded to the Park Service in 2011.

During the summers of 2012 and 2013, the Park Service teamed up with a other groups to create a buffer space of fire-resistant landscape around each of the structures on the island. Over 100 trees were removed which allowed Baker Island Lighthouse to function again as an effective aid to navigation.

More information on the current state of renovations on the island can be found at this link, hosted by the Keepers of Baker Island:

http://www.keepersofbakerisland.org/

Best Viewing

The lighthouse grounds are open to the public during summer months. The light is not visible from mainland points and must be visited by boat.

Bar Harbor Whale Watch Co. offers periodic cruises of many lighthouses, including Baker Island Light. For more information, visit: *https://www.barharborwhales.com/*

***

52 Bear Island Light

Year Established: 1839
Nearest to: Northeast Harbor
Latitude: 44° 17' 00" N
Longitude: 68° 16' 11" W
Tower Height: 31ft
Elevation: 100ft
Design: Tapered Cylindrical Tower
1st Designer(s): Unknown (1839)
2nd Designer(s): Unknown (1852)
3rd Designer(s): U.S. Army Corp of Engineering (1889)
Material: Brick
Light Sequence: White light – 5 sec. on – repeating
Fog Horn: No fog signal

Source: National Archives

National Register of Historic Places (01/05/1988)

Physical Appearance:

Sited above a bold rock ledge, Bear Island Light Station is composed of a squat tower with an attached workroom, a detached, frame gambrel roofed keeper's house, a barn, a diminutive stone oil house and a boathouse.

The light tower is constructed of brick and has a slightly tapered configuration. A pair of small window openings in the shaft provide interior illumination. Its polygonal lantern, which no longer shelters a beacon, is framed by a relatively wide circular parapet that is supported by iron brackets and bordered by a railing. The attached ancillary brick building has a single window on both side walls and a door in the gable end. This tower and workroom date to 1889 when the entire station was rebuilt.

A short distance to the northeast of the tower is the one-and-a-half-story keeper's quarters. The rectangular dwelling is sheathed in clapboards and wood shingles in the gambrel ends. Its three-bay front elevation is symmetrically composed with a central door flanked by window openings (since boarded over). Two small dormers punctuate the roof and a pair of brick flues rise through the ridge. There are four windows on both ends; two on each story. A small shed roofed addition with three windows and a door is attached to the rear. Above it is another dormer. The present dwelling replaces the original one-and-a-half -story stone building and its low one-story frame ell.

The first complex built at Bear Island in 1839 employed a stone dwelling surmounted by a lantern. In 1852, a brick tower was erected off one end of the dwelling, and in 1889 the entire complex was pulled down and rebuilt. This chronology of construction is an important reminder of the constant historic process of the rebuilding and upgrading of Maine's light stations.

Historical Significance:

Bear Island Light Station was established in 1839 as a guide to Northeast Harbor on Mount Desert Island. It is prominently located at the summit and western end of Bear Island.

Additional Information

Bear Island Lighthouse resides at the southern entrance to Northeast Harbor on Mount Desert Island. Bear Island might have originally been named "Bare," due to its lack of trees, since it is doubtful the island was ever home to any bears.

In 1852, a fire damaged the original 1839 light tower, and in 1854, the tower was rebuilt. The new lighthouse consisted of a round brick tower at one end of the dwelling. It appears that much of the original structure was salvaged during the rebuilding.

By 1888, the rebuilt tower was in poor shape. As a result, the present 31-foot brick lighthouse was built in 1889–90 after a congressional appropriation of $3,750, as were a new one-and-one-half-story, wood-frame keeper's house and a barn.

Once the light was deactivated by the Coast Guard and replaced by two lighted bell buoys anchored offshore in 1961, Bear Island Lighthouse slowly began to deteriorate.

The National Park Service was granted ownership of the station in 1987, and not long thereafter, the Friends of Acadia renovated the lighthouse. A marine light was added in 1989 and the lighthouse was approved as a private aid to navigation, exhibiting a white flash every five seconds.

Once the lighthouse was listed on the National Register of Historic Places in 1988, the Park Service was permitted to lease the property. A long-term lease was granted on the property to a professor from Georgetown University, on the condition that he pay for the upkeep of the property. The property remains in private hands today.

Best Viewing

Bear Island Light is located approximately 1/3 mile offshore from Mount Desert Island, nearest to the town of Northeast Harbor. Remote views can be made from Shore Road in Manset.

The best views of Bear Island Light are from the water. Bar Harbor Whale Watch Co. offers periodic cruises of many lighthouses around Mount Desert Island. For more information:

https://www.barharborwhales.com/

53 Egg Rock Light

Year Established: 1875
Nearest to: Winter Harbor
Latitude: 44° 21' 14" N
Longitude: 68° 08' 18" W
Tower Height: 40ft
Elevation: 64ft
Design: Square Tower

Source: National Archives

Designer(s): U.S. Army Corps of Engineers (1875)
Material: Brick
Light Sequence: Red light – 5 sec. on – repeating
Fog Horn: Two blasts every 30 seconds

National Register of Historic Places (12/07/1987)

Physical Appearance:

The Egg Rock Light Station has one of the most unusual configurations of extant light complexes in Maine: a square brick tower rises through the center of a one-and-a-half-story square, hip roofed frame keeper's dwelling. Of the four original ancillary buildings on this site only the rectangular brick fog signal building survives.

Constructed in 1875, the dwelling has a three-bay facade composed of a centrally-located door flanked by window openings (which have since been covered). A long shed roofed dormer with pent gables at the corners and four openings is attached to the high hip roof on this elevation. This pattern is repeated on the east elevation. Both side walls feature a trio of window openings and coupled gable roofed dormers. Chimneys punctuate the roof on both of these elevations. The tower stairwell is illuminated by a single window on the west side. A metal railing frames the tower and its octagonal aluminum lantern, a 1986 replacement of the structure which had been removed some years earlier. In 1899 the Annual Report of the Light-House Board proposed that the dwelling at Egg Rock be enlarged with a half-story addition to the roof. Documentary photographs show that this change radically altered the roof profile from the original shallow hip to a high hip with dormers.

Historical Significance:

Egg Rock Light Station, situated on a bold rock island at the entrance to Frenchman Bay, is the only extant complex of this configuration in Maine.

The light station on Egg Rock is prominently located in Frenchman Bay between Mount Desert Island to the west and Schoodic Peninsula to the east. Its construction here was undoubtedly in response to the rising maritime traffic in the bay, a large proportion of which was increasingly associated with summer tourism in and around Bar Harbor.

The establishment of a steam powered fog signal in 1904 further underlines the importance of the station to local traffic. Egg Rock was automated by the Coast Guard in 1976, and its ancillary buildings, with the exception of the fog signal, were subsequently pulled down.

Additional Information

Originally, Egg Rock Light was a rare example of a twelve-foot square, brick tower rising from the center of a square, nearly-flat-roofed keeper's dwelling.

Instead of the usual spiral staircase found in other light towers, the stairs leading to the lantern room follow the square contours of the building.

In June 1904, in apparent response to the grounding of battleship *USS Massachusetts* on a ledge near Egg Rock, the fog signal horn received a major upgrade. Complaints by local summer residents, including noted newspaper publisher Joseph Pulitzer, led Maine Senator Eugene Hale to send a telegram to the Lighthouse Board, requesting relief from the loud fog signal. The Board responded in July 1904, with some disdain for the residents:

"There is much truth in the story from Bar Harbor and some exaggeration. This fog horn is simply carrying out the mandates of Congress....This conflict between shore dwellers and the mariners has always been with us, and is one of the most difficult situations the department has to face. As the board is created, however, to give protection to the mariner, his interests are to be conserved first, and the summer cottagers who live two months in the year in the vicinity of the station will be given such consideration as is proper."

Eventually, cooler heads prevailed when the Chairman of the Lighthouse Board arrived in Maine to personally assess the situation. By 1905, the fog horn had been turned away from Bar Harbor, reducing the onshore noise, and the complaints from residents.

In 1976, the Coast Guard removed the lantern room from the tower to make room for rotating aero-beacon, creating what many called "the ugliest lighthouse in Maine." It received so many complaints that in 1986, the Coast Guard built an aluminum lantern room to house a modern optic, powered by an underwater cable from Mount Desert Island.

In 1998, Egg Rock Light was one of six Maine light stations transferred to the U.S. Fish & Wildlife Service, and managed as part of the Maine Coastal Islands National Wildlife Refuge.

https://www.fws.gov/refuge/Maine_Coastal_Islands/about/lighthouses.html

In 2009, the U.S. Fish & Wildlife Service was able to provide federal funds for economic stimulus to provide materials for a community-led repair mission.

As one of the most-viewed lights in Maine, this attracted the attention of residents and area businesses that donated their time, money, and materials to help the project.

Best Viewing

Egg Rock Light is located at the entrance to Frenchman Bay, nearest to the town of Winter Harbor. The light is visible from a distance at scenic points along Park Loop Road in Acadia National Park, and from atop Cadillac Mountain.

The best views of Egg Rock Light are from the water. Bar Harbor Whale Watch Co. offers periodic cruises of many lighthouses around Mount Desert Island. For more information: *https://www.barharborwhales.com/*

54 Winter Harbor Light (Mark Island Light)

Year Established: 1857
Nearest to: Winter Harbor
Latitude: 44° 21' 41" N
Longitude: 68° 05' 16" W
Tower Height: 19ft
Elevation: 37ft
Design: Cylindrical Tower

Source: U.S. Coast Guard

Designer(s): U.S. Army Corps of Engineers (1857)
Material: Brick
Light Sequence: No light signal
Fog Horn: No fog signal

National Register of Historic Places (12/21/1987)

Physical Appearance:

The Winter Harbor Light Station consists of a cylindrical brick tower connected to the one-story ell of the frame keeper's house by means of a narrow brick workroom.

A small frame wood shingled shed stands to the northeast of the dwelling, and an oil house and boathouse are located to the north.

Typical of mid-nineteenth century light towers, the brick structure rests on a short granite foundation and is capped by an iron walkway with attached railing. It was erected in 1856. There is a single six-over-six double-hung sash window on the east face of the tower. The original octagonal lantern with its domed polygonal roof and spherical ventilator survives.

The connecting workroom has a door on its east elevation and a window on the west side. Doors flanked by a pair of windows form the original fenestration pattern on both sides of the ell. A shed roofed asymmetrical three-bay addition has since been added to the east elevation. The two-story house, which is sheathed in clapboards, features four six-over-six double-hung sash windows on both gable ends and two windows on the north facade. This dwelling and its long connecting ell were built in 1876 to replace the original house.

Historical Significance:

Winter Harbor Light Station was established in 1856 on Mark Island as a guide to nearby Winter and Mosquito harbors.

The light station on Mark Island served in an important capacity as a primary navigational aid to the local fishing fleet as well as nearby maritime transportation routes. This latter point became increasingly significant in the late nineteenth century as the development of the summer tourist industry on Mount Desert Island increased the number of pleasure craft that plied the waterways in the area. This light was decommissioned in 1934 and sold to a private citizen.

Additional Information

Winter Harbor Light was considered to be a good assignment, housing only nine keepers and their families in its 76-year span from 1857 until 1933. Unfortunately, like many other light stations of the 1930s, the Coast Guard deemed the light to be unnecessary and offered it for sale at auction once it was decommissioned.

In 1934, a Bar Harbor man bought the property at auction for $552. Three years later, Bernice Richmond, a writer and musician, purchased the island from the original owner. Richmond, originally from Livermore

Falls, later wrote about at her experiences at Winter Island Light in a book titled *Our Island Lighthouse*.

In the 1950s, the island was sold to another author. This time to Rene Prud'hommeaux, an author of many children's novels, including *The Sunken Forest* and *The Port of Missing Men*. Prud'hommeaux's wife, Patricia, wrote a children's novel loosely based on Winter Harbor Light, titled *The Light in the Tower*, under the name Joan Howard.

The book describes a lighthouse much like the Winter Harbor Light, but unlike the actual light, in the book the lighthouse is relighted, thanks to a caring young boy.

Since then, the island and light station has been sold to a string of individuals: a playwright, a financial consultant, and an interior designer. As of 2019, the property is again listed for sale. During its time in private ownership, Winter Harbor Light has been in various states of repair and despair. Given that the current listing price is north of $2 million, it can be assumed that the property is in reasonably good condition.

Best Viewing

Winter Harbor Light is located on Mark Island near the town of Winter Harbor. The lighthouse is not accessible to the public but can be seen distantly from the Park Loop Road on Acadia National Park's Schoodic Peninsula.

The best views of Winter Harbor Light are from the water. Bar Harbor Whale Watch Co. offers periodic cruises of many lighthouses around Mount Desert Island. For more information:

https://www.barharborwhales.com/

***

55 Prospect Harbor Light

Year Established: 1850
Nearest to: Prospect Harbor
Latitude: 44° 24' 12" N
Longitude: 68° 00' 46" W
Tower Height: 38ft
Elevation: 42ft

Source: National Historic Register

Design: Conical Tower
1st Designer(s): Unknown (1850)
2nd Designer(s): U.S. Army Corps of Engineers (1891)
Material: Wood
Light Sequence: Red or white light, depending on heading – 6 sec. on – repeating
Fog Horn:

National Register of Historic Places (01/02/1988)

Physical Appearance:

Prospect Harbor Light Station consists of a conical tower and a detached one-and-a-half-story frame keeper's house. Some distance to the north of the dwelling is a small stone gable roofed oil house. The station occupies a shallow rocky peninsula.

The handsome shingled light tower at Prospect Harbor features a door on its north face and a pedimented window opening in the west side. It was erected in 1891. A covered passageway that sheltered the door and linked the house and tower has been removed. A circular iron walkway with railing caps the tower. Rising from the middle of the deck is a ten-sided lantern with a polygonal roof and spherical ventilator.

Facing west across Prospect Harbor, the 1891 keeper's house has an asymmetrical five-bay facade partially sheltered by an engaged shed roofed porch. Its first story is sheathed in clapboards and its upper floor in wood shingles. Four square posts linked by a slat balustrade support the porch roof above which is a large gable roofed dormer. The windows on the first story and in the dormer employ four-over-four double hung sash. A brick flue and one chimney punctuate the roof. There are two windows, one on each story, in the gable ends. There are a number of openings on the rear elevation and a small addition at the southeast corner of the house.

At the time of its establishment in 1850 the station consisted of a granite tower attached to one end of a stone dwelling. In 1870 these buildings were rehabilitated, and 1891 they were pulled down and replaced by the existing components.

Historical Significance:

Authorized in 1847 but not established until 1850, the Prospect Harbor Light Station marks the eastern entrance to the inner section of this harbor of refuge.

The light station at Prospect Harbor was built in response to the local need for a navigational aid to this deep and sheltered anchorage. Throughout the nineteenth century Prospect Harbor was home to a large fleet of fishing vessels whose safe passage in and around the harbor was greatly facilitated by the beacon and fog signal at this location. However, despite this apparent need for the station, the Light-House Board deactivated the light in 1859 claiming that the harbor was not used as an anchorage during storms. In 1870, for some as yet unknown reason, the light was relit and the buildings renovated.

Additional Information

The original 1850 lighthouse was a granite conical tower attached to a one-and-a-half-story granite keeper's dwelling.

Congress decided to discontinue Prospect Harbor Light in 1859 after being informed that the harbor was "not used as a harbor of refuge" and the nearby village had only a little coasting trade, which did not justify the maintenance of the light.

This decision was reversed roughly a decade later, and the light was re-established "to serve as a guide to the harbor of refuge which it marks." The existing tower, lantern room, and keeper's dwelling were thoroughly renovated and repaired and a few new out-buildings put in place.

Despite extensive repairs made in 1881 to the tower and house, by 1889 the stone dwelling and tower were reported to be in "poor condition."

Subsequently, in 1891, a conical, wooden light tower, thirty-eight feet tall, was built about twenty-five feet south of the original granite lighthouse, which was dismantled.

The wooden light tower, which still stands today, is 38 feet from base to lantern, and the light shines 42 feet above the mean sea level.

In May 2000, the American Lighthouse Foundation assumed responsibility for Prospect Harbor Lighthouse from the Coast Guard. According to a Coast Guard spokesman:

"I think that partnership, I like to call it, when we lease or license a light out to a group, is just great for that

light. They can put more money into a tower than what we have and ultimately end up with a better looking structure while the Coast Guard can focus on maintaining the signal for the mariner."

By the time the lighthouse was transferred to the Foundation, the tower was facing serious structural deterioration. Without the combined efforts of the Coast Guard, the American Lighthouse Foundation, the New England Lighthouse Lovers, and many concerned citizens, Prospect Harbor Lighthouse might not exist today.

Years of water damage on the timber platform supporting the lantern room and the spiral staircase winding up to it were rotted through, almost causing one of the last remaining wooden conical towers in the United States to completely collapse.

From 2001 to 2004, the American Lighthouse Foundation initiated a major renovation of the light tower, including the removal of the lantern and gallery by crane in order to replace its supporting deck and timbers. Other interior and exterior improvements were made: shingling, repainting, repairing, and replacement of the staircase and ladder leading to the lantern room.

Today Prospect Harbor Light stands firmly as additional restoration work continues.

Best Viewing

Prospect Harbor Light is located on an active U.S. Navy base and is not open to the public for security reasons. A good view of the light is available at the entrance of the Navy installation on Lighthouse Point Road in Prospect Harbor. There are no real parking spaces; pull to the side of the road. Active duty and retired military personal can stay at the keeper's house, known as the *"Gull Cottage"*. For more information:

http://www.militarycampgrounds.us/maine/gull-cottage-at-prospect-harbor

***

56 Petit Manan Light

Year Established: 1817
Nearest to: Corea
Latitude: 44° 22' 03" N
Longitude: 67° 51' 51" W
Tower Height: 119ft
Elevation: 123ft
Design: Conical Tower

Source: National Archives

1st Designer(s): Fredrick&William Polk, Mr. Dearborn (1817)
2nd Designer(s): US Army Corps of Engineers (1855)
Material: Granite Block
Light Sequence: White light – 10 sec. on – repeating
Fog Horn: One blast every 30 seconds

National Register of Historic Places (09/25/1987)

Physical Appearance:

Petit Manan Light Station is located on Petit Manan Island, a rocky and windblown site 2 miles from the mainland. Contributing features include the keeper's dwelling, rain shed, generator building, paint locker, and boat house. The light tower is of unusual height for the period of construction and of impressive appearance. The remaining buildings are vernacular in appearance, typical of their period and function, and constitute an unusually complete complex.

The first light on Petit Manan was commissioned on April 27, 1816, and the island was acquired on June 15, 1816, from the Commonwealth of Massachusetts. The first tower was 25 feet in height and was located several yards south of the present tower. The station at that time consisted of a rubblestone keeper's dwelling, frame privy, and rubblestone light. The tower contained 13 whale oil lamps (probably Argand cylindrical wicks) each with a 15 inch reflector. The focal plane was 53 feet above sea level and could be seen for 14 miles. It was completed in 1817.

The tower was extensively rebuilt between 1823 and 1825, with the number of lamps reduced to eight, (having 9-inch reflectors). In 1843 the number of lamps was again increased to 13. In 1852, a 1,200-pound, hand-rung brass fog bell was installed. A photograph (probably dated 1870) shows the old tower still in place; however, an 1889 photograph does not show the old tower. It presumably was torn down to provide stone foundations for the several buildings built during this period. In 1876 and 1899 cellars were dug for the two dwellings and rubblestone foundations constructed, possibly out of the old tower and dwelling.

The present light tower, constructed of ashlar masonry was commissioned by the U.S. Lighthouse Board in 1854 and completed in 1855 by the Corps of Engineers. It was built of local granite quarried on the mainland. The circular stone tower is 109 feet high, 20 feet in diameter at the base, and 12 feet in diameter at the top. It is topped by a two-story, 12-sided iron and glass lantern and watch room, giving the light itself a focal plane of 123 feet—the second highest in Maine. The cast iron capping was added to the tower in 1882. The original cast iron gargoyles were removed prior to automation; one is on display at the Shore Village Museum in Rockland.

The interior of the tower is lined with brick, with a cast iron spiral staircase containing 147 steps. Eighteen of the steps were damaged in 1869 when a chain holding the weights broke. The repairs to the steps can still be seen.

Following a series of unusually strong storms (1856 and 1886) which loosened the top two courses of the tower, six sets of one and one/half inch tie rods were added to the exterior for stabilization, in the summer of 1887. Similar repairs were performed at the same time at Boon Island Light, the tallest in Maine, which had been built 1852 to similar design.

There were originally 11 windows in the tower. The bottom two have been bricked up to prevent unauthorized entry. The remaining nine contain structural glass block "panes".

The lens was a second order Fresnel lens (having 27.6" between flame and lens), manufactured by Henri Lepante of Paris. Originally, a fixed light fueled by whale oil lamps, it had a 17-mile visibility. In 1857 it was converted to a "fixed light varied by flashes", caused by three panels revolving on belt driven chariot wheels, driven by a system of pulleys and weights that had to be hand wound every five and one-half hours. The panels made one complete rotation every six minutes; therefore, every 110 seconds there would be a 10-second "pause" as a panel obscured the light.

A 1 1/2 story Greek Revival style frame double house was built at the same time as the present tower. A new cellar was built for the house and it was moved several yards north in 1899. It was torn down in the 1950's. The later cellar hole is still present, partially filled with debris.

A second keeper's dwelling was built in 1876. It is a single family, two story frame house with asbestos shingles over the original clapboards. It is approximately 24 x 30 feet over a full rubblestone cellar. It contains four rooms on the first floor: a kitchen with storm porch, pantry, living room, front hallway with storm porch; and four rooms on the second floor: three bedrooms and a bath.

The dwelling and ancillary structures were turned over to the U.S. Fish and Wildlife Service in 1974 and have been unoccupied since. Unsecured for 10 years, the dwelling was secured with plywood shutters in 1984. It was cleaned out and minor repairs were made in 1984 and 1985 to prevent further deterioration.

Historical Significance:

The original light station on Petit Manan Island was completed in 1817. The importance of this location is demonstrated by that fact that this was the 8th light built in Maine, of 66 eventually constructed, and the 37th in the U.S., out of 1,600. This first light was visible at 14 miles, used metal reflectors, and appears to have been typical of many early American lights in its construction and equipment.

Investigations by the newly created Lighthouse Board in the early 1850s revealed the inadequacy of American lighthouses, both in number and design. The Petit Manan Light was found to be both too weak and too low in focal plane (53 feet) considering the ever-increasing use of the Northern shipping lanes during this period. Therefore a new light tower with a Fresnel lens was commissioned in 1854, accompanied by a replacement of the ancilliary buildings comprising the station.

This is the present light tower completed in 1855. With a focal plane of 123 feet, the imposing granite tower has been a very important light, serving not only local fishermen and boaters, but also the offshore shipping and fishing industries. Petit Manan has undoubtedly had an impact on safety of ships on the coast. It is the first light seen by ships from Canada or Europe using the northern shipping lanes.

As such, it guided substantial numbers of vessels in international traffic. It also guided coastal vessels entering five local bays in an area noted during the period of significance for shipbuilding, timber harvest, and fishing industries; and guided local fishermen in their daily routine.

The need for a light at this location is further demonstrated by the fact that prior to 1935, 27 vessels are recorded as needing assistance within sight of the light, including two captured and burned by the Confederate raider Alabama during the Civil War. Most of these vessels were coastal cargo and fishing schooners, indicative of the volume of this traffic along the Maine coast during this period, but a few more unusual vessels also wrecked nearby (such as the early paddle steamer "New York", which burned and sank in 1826). The relatively early installation of a fog signal (1869) is also indicative of the importance of this light and hazards of the area. (In 1880, over 70% of America's light stations had still not been so equipped).

During World Wars I and II, Petit Manan was particularly important to coastal defense as a lookout tower for foreign ships and submarines, due to its location 2 miles off the mainland.

Petit Manan Light Station is today one of the most complete examples of an island light station on the Maine Coast. It includes examples of all the essential ancillary buildings of a late 19th century island station and (with the exception of the demolished 1855 keeper's dwelling) and a few minor outbuildings appears substantially as it did during the period of significance.

The light tower is one of the 4 tallest in New England, and the second highest in Maine. As such, it reflects state of the art design at the time of construction.

The tower at Boon Island Light Station is the only one of these similar in date and design, and both exhibited the same construction flaws necessitating repairs in 1887. There have been no notable alterations to the exterior of the tower since that date although the light mechanism has undergone the series of necessary modernizations typical of an active station.

The remaining buildings at this station are typical of vernacular structures built by the Lighthouse Service during the last quarter of the 19th century. Again, while all have undergone modernization and use changes in the 20th century, their exterior have never undergone significant modification. The electrification of the station in 1938 decreased the need for some of the ancillary structures, and all were made obsolete by automation of the light in 1972. Because of these modernizations to the light, the ancillary structures remained essentially as they appeared between 1876 and 1937, with some deterioration due to weather conditions coupled with only limited maintenance since 1972.

Additional Information

Petit Manan Island was named by explorer Samuel de Champlain since the island reminded him of Grand Manan Island, located to the northeast in New Brunswick, Canada.

"Manan" appears to be a derivative of "mun-an-ook" or "man-an-ook", meaning "island place", from the Maliseet-Passamaquoddy-Penobscot tribes.

The Petit Manan light station has a history of odd occurrences by its keepers. In one instance, an 1831 surprise inspection revealed that the lighthouse was in very poor condition and that other structures were "positively dirty." Upon further discussion, it was revealed that the keeper, who may have been ill, had left his wife in charge of upkeep, without informing anyone of his decision.

The keeper was quickly dismissed, and he died a year later. His wife applied for the now vacant position, but it was awarded instead another person.

In another instance, in December 1916, the lighthouse keeper left the island in a powerboat to pick up his wife, who was visiting with her parents at Moose Peak Light. Unfortunately, his boat appeared to have capsized in heavy seas; a later search found the empty boat but the keeper was never found.

After the light was automated by the Coast Guard in the 1970s, Petit Manan Island, except for the light tower, was transferred in 1974 to the U.S. Fish and Wildlife Service. It became part of the 3,335-acre Petit Manan National Wildlife Refuge.

Petit Manan Lighthouse was listed for transfer in 2004 under the National Historic Lighthouse Preservation Act of 2000. Four nonprofit groups as well as the U.S. Fish and Wildlife Service applied for the lighthouse. In late 2006, complete ownership of the island, including the light tower, was transferred to the Fish and Wildlife Service.

The island is now part of the Maine Coastal Islands National Wildlife Refuge. The former keeper's quarters now house refuge personnel, who perform regular research duties in addition to helping maintain the light station.

https://www.fws.gov/refuge/maine_coastal_islands/

Best Viewing

This light is located off Petit Manan Point, nearest to the town of Corea. This location is considered one of the foggiest on the Maine coast, with approximately 70 foggy days per year.

The lighthouse can be viewed from a distance from Petit Manan Point in Milbridge, reached by a two-mile hike along Shore Trail.

Puffin watch cruises out of Bar Harbor go close to Petit Manan Island for an excellent view of its feathered residents as well as the lighthouse. For example, *Acadian Boat Tours* of Bar Harbor offers scenic cruises past Petit Manan: *https://acadianboattours.com/*

According to their website:

"Offering a 3.5-hour "Puffins, Lighthouses and Seabirds" trip, leaving daily at 12:30 p.m. from Bar Harbor, late May to late October. Includes viewing of Winter Harbor (Mark Island), Petit Manan, and Egg Rock Lighthouses. This trip includes an extended viewing of Petit Manan Lighthouse, one of only seven islands in Maine where endangered Atlantic Puffins nest."

57 Narraguagus Light (Pond Island Light)

Year Established: 1853
Nearest to: Millbridge
Latitude: 44° 27' 12" N
Longitude: 67° 49' 56" W
Tower Height: 31ft
Elevation: 54ft
Design: Cylindrical Tower
Designer(s): US Army Corps of Engineers (1853)
Material: Brick
Light Sequence: No light signal
Fog Horn: No fog signal

Source: National Historic Register

National Register of Historic Places (10/13/1987)

Physical Appearance:

Occupying a rock ledge on the east side of Pond Island, the Narraguagus Light Station consists of a circular brick tower joined to a frame keeper's house by way of an L-shaped workroom. Frame sheds stand to the north and west of the dwelling.

The light tower rises to a height of nearly thirty-one feet from its base to the center of the lantern. Erected in 1853 and reinforced in 1894 with additional brick masonry, the tower shaft is punctuated by a trio of two-over-two double-hung sash windows. It is capped by an iron deck and railing. This is the third deck known to have been put into service here. The original was replaced in 1876 and that one was upgraded in 1894. The ten sided lantern, dating to 1876, is covered by a polygonal roof that is surmounted by a spherical ventilator. Its lens has been removed. In 1887 the larger north wing, which is a remnant of the original dwelling, was converted to a workroom. A cellar and cistern were built beneath it, and a second brick ell constructed to link the house and tower.

Projecting to the west of the tower, the keeper's house is a one-and-a-half story wooden frame building constructed in 1875. It features an enclosed porch on its east gable end, label moldings at the windows and a central brick flue. The house is sheathed in clapboards.

When originally constructed in 1853 this station contained a five-bay dwelling surmounted by a centrally placed light tower. This resembled those structures constructed earlier at Grindle Point and Indian Island. In 1875 the new house was built but the tower remained in place on the original dwelling (which was probably brick). Nine years later a portion of this house was removed and the tower was left exposed at one end. Finally, in 1894, the diameter of the tower was increased to its present size. The station was deactivated in 1934 and sold to a private citizen.

Historical Significance:

The Narraguagus Light Station was established in 1853 as a guide to navigation in and around Narraguagus Bay. It was built during the most active period of lighthouse construction in Maine which followed the organization of the Lighthouse Board in 1852.

This light station was the primary nineteenth century navigational aid to Narraguagus Bay. Milbridge, located at the north end of the bay, was a locally important coastal community whose deep harbor was the site of an active ship building industry. Situated at the head of navigation on the Narraguagus River, the town was also the shipping point for lumber manufactures located upriver, principally at Cherryfield. These principal activities were augmented by other maritime related industries such as fishing, coasting and lobster processing.

Additional Information

According to lore, Narraguagus was a word used by Native Americans that meant "wide and shallow," and it has been applied to both a river and bay in the areas surrounding Milbridge. Starting inland at Eagle Lake, the Narraguagus River runs southeast for 55 miles to Milbridge, where it empties into Narraguagus Bay.

In the mid-1800s, Milbridge was an important shipbuilding center, rivaling Bath with over 150 large ships launched into the river from the town's shipyards.

There are at least ten islands in Maine named "Pond Island," including one in Georgetown that is home to another light station. To avoid confusion, the Lighthouse Board decided to officially name the 2nd Pond Island Light as Narraguagus Light. Locals, preferring familiar names, simply refer to this lighthouse as *Pond Island Light*.

An inn, which still exists today, was built on the island in 1878 and a golf course was added in the 1920s. With these amenities, the island became something of a mini-resort. During this period, it has been reported that on Sundays, people would gather at the lighthouse keeper's home for evening hymn-singing sessions, enriched by a pump organ played by the keeper's wife.

Narraguagus Light was discontinued by the Coast Guard in 1934, and the lighthouse and other buildings and the surrounding five acres were sold at auction to a private citizen. The property has reported been passed down through this family and is believed to still be owned by them. A lighted buoy, located just off Pond Island, has replaced the function of the lighthouse.

Best Viewing

This lighthouse is located on Pond Island in Narraguagus Bay, nearest to the town of Millbridge. The light is not visible from mainland point nor is it accessible to the public. *Robertson Sea Tours* in Milbridge offers periodic cruises to Narraguagas Light and other nearby light stations:

http://www.robertsonseatours.com/lighthouse-tours/

From their website:

"This is a 3 hour cruise which visits the 3 local Light Houses closest to Narraguagus Bay. Narraguagus Lighthouse located on Pond Island, Petit Manan Lighthouse located on Petit Manan Island. Our puffin and Seabird Cruises visit this Island during the summer, it is a wildlife refuge and the Light House tower is the second tallest in Maine. The third Lighthouse is Nash Island light located on Nash Island. Also During the trip Seals, Eagles and Scenic coastline may also be viewed."

58 Nash Island Light

Year Established: 1838
Nearest to: Addison
Latitude: 44° 27' 51" N
Longitude: 67° 44' 50" W
Tower Height: 29ft
Elevation: 51ft
Design: Square Tapered Tower
1st Designer(s): Unknown (1838)
2nd Designer(s): Unknown (1874)
Material: Brick
Light Sequence: No light signal
Fog Horn: No fog signal

Source: National Archives

Lighthouse Appearance and History

Nash Island Light is one of only ten Maine lighthouses which are not registered with the National Register of Historic Places.

In 1837, Congress authorized the construction of a lighthouse at the mouth of the Pleasant River. The site chosen was Nash Island. At that time, many towns along the river including Colombia, Colombia Falls, and Addison were active with shipbuilding coastal trade and the export of lumber, granite, and fish.

The government purchased approximately four acres of land for the station from the Nash family, for which the island was named. During 1838, the first Nash Island Lighthouse, a 24-foot-tall conical rubblestone tower was constructed, along with a simple rubblestone keeper's dwelling.

Just five years later, in 1843, it was reported that the lantern roof was leaky and the east side of the tower was badly cracked.

In subsequent years, major repairs were made to the lighthouse, including the replacement of the lighthouse's original lamps and reflectors with a fourth-order Fresnel lens in 1856.

Despite these repairs, as early as 1857, the tower was so badly storm damaged that the Lighthouse Board's annual report recommended complete rebuilding, reasoning that repairs would have been more costly than the value of the existing building.

By 1874, the original tower was demolished completely rebuilt. This 51-foot square tapered brick lighthouse still stands today. In 1888, a bell tower with a 1,000 pound fog bell was added.

In 1947, the Coast Guard destroyed all of the dwellings, the fog signal building, the oil house, and the boathouse and landing ramps, leaving the tower alone.

The light was discontinued in 1982 and replaced by an offshore buoy. The Coast Guard had planned to destroy the lighthouse tower as well, but due to public outcry, it was left standing.

A small nonprofit group, the *Friends of Nash Island Light*, applied for the property in 1996 under the Maine Lights Program. In December 1997 the Maine Lighthouse Selection Committee announced the transfer of the lighthouse to the nonprofit group. Since then, the Friends of Nash Island Light completed significant restoration work on the lighthouse. For more information on their restoration progress, visit: *https://nashislandlight.org/*

Best Viewing

Nash Island Light is located on Nash Island at the Southeast entrance to the mouth of Pleasant Bay, nearest to the town of Addison. Nash Island is part of the Petit Manan Wildlife Refuge, and is closed to the public to protect nesting seabirds during the summer months. Nash Island has been designated by the U.S. Fish and Wildlife Service as an area for migratory birds.

The lighthouse is not visible from mainland locations and is best viewed by boat. As mentioned with regard to Narraguagus Light, *Robertson Sea Tours* in Milbridge offers periodic cruises to Nash Island Light and other nearby light stations:

http://www.robertsonseatours.com/lighthouse-tours/

***

59 Moose Peak Light

Year Established: 1826
Nearest to: Jonesport
Latitude: 44° 28' 28" N
Longitude: 67° 31' 55" W
Tower Height: 57ft
Elevation: 72ft
Design: Conical Tower
Designer(s): Jeremiah Berry (1826)
Material: Brick
Light Sequence: White light – 30 sec. on - repeating
Fog Horn: 2 blasts every 30 seconds

Source: National Archives

Lighthouse Appearance and History

Moose Peak Light is one of only ten Maine lighthouses which are not registered with the National Register of Historic Places.

In 1825, Congress approved the construction of a light at the entrance to Englishman Bay. Mistake Island, a 30-acre island five miles south Jonesport was chosen as the location of the light station. Not only marking the bay entrance, Moose Peak Light also marked the primary coastal shipping channel known as *Main Channel Way*.

A 24-foot-tall round granite rubblestone tower was constructed on three acres of the island, and a rubblestone dwelling was built some 300 feet from the tower. The lighthouse was topped by a wrought-iron lantern, seven feet high, with a copper dome. A wooden footbridge made it possible to walk across a chasm between the house and the tower.

According to records, the tower was "refitted" in 1851 with the installation of a new lantern room and the construction of a new brick external lining, raising the focal plane of the light 12 feet to a height of 65 feet.

The lighthouse was fitted with a second-order Fresnel lens in 1856. The tower developed cracks in the years that followed, apparently because inferior mortar was used in the 1851 construction.

By 1885, the tower's foundation was cracked due to settling, while the tower itself had bulged out in places with cracks that ran its entire length. An 1885 report from the Lighthouse Board noted:

"The tower, which was built in 1826, has been repeatedly pointed and repaired, but from defects in its construction it cannot be made safe. A new tower should be built, as near as practicable to the present one."

Congress appropriated the requested amount on August 4, 1886 for "rebuilding the tower at Moose Peak Light-Station," however, there is some ambiguity over whether the tower was rebuilt or reconstructed in 1888.

What is known is that the 1888 tower now had a focal plane of seventy-two feet and a new lantern room. In 1901, an eight-inch-thick covering of brick masonry was put in place to further reinforce the tower.

In 1912, a fog signal house was erected with a powerful diaphragm fog horn. During the period from 1918 to 1934, the keepers at Moose Peak Light logged more hours of dense fog than any other Maine light station.

Moose Peak Light was automated in 1972 and the Fresnel lens was replaced by an acrylic optic.

In 1982, a military team, most likely the 10th Special Forces Group from Massachusetts that had performed similar operations at Saddleback Ledge Light in 1960 and at Two Bush Light in 1969, blew up the keeper's house as a training exercise.

In 2010, the Coast Guard announced that Moose Peak Lighthouse would be made available at no cost to eligible community organizations. The Town of Jonesport formed the non-profit group *Keepers of Moose Peak Light*, which submitted an application to acquire the lighthouse. In 2012, the organization learned that their application for the lighthouse had been denied due to lack of funding by the group.

The lighthouse, four surrounding acres, and the station's boathouse were offered at auction in 2012. Five bidders participated in the auction, which closed on November 1, 2012, with a winning bid awarded to a Connecticut man. In a curious move, the man in 2017 donated the lighthouse to a Jonesport nonprofit that specializes in providing buildings to health care providers. It is not known if any improvements have been made to the structure since the 2012 auction.

Best Viewing

This lighthouse is located on Mistake Island, nearest to the town of Jonesport. This light is not accessible to the public and is best viewed by boat cruises in the area.

Moose Peak Light, an active aid to navigation, is not visible from the mainland. In this remote area, scheduled lighthouse cruises are infrequent.

Bar Harbor Whale Watch offers a yearly "Grand Slam" 18-lighthouse tour that includes Moose Peak Light. For more information: https://www.barharborwhales.com

***

60 Libby Island Light

Year Established: 1822
Nearest to: Machiasport
Latitude: 44° 34' 05" N
Longitude: 67° 22' 02" W
Tower Height: 42ft
Elevation: 91ft
Design: Conical Tower

Source: National Archives

1st Designer(s): Benjamin Beal / Quincy Bicknel (1822)
2nd Designer(s): Alexander Parris, Noah Humphrey (1824)
Material: Granite Block
Light Sequence: White light – 20 sec. on - repeating
Fog Horn: 1 blast every 15 seconds

National Register of Historic Places (05/01/1976)

Physical Appearance:

Libby Island Light Station is located on the island's southwestern part and marks the entrance to Machais Bay. The tower is built of granite, in a conical design, white in color. 42' high, built in 1819, basically unaltered, 91' above sea level. The tower's base diameter is 16' and at the parapet is 12'4". Dwelling built in 1824, 34' x 36' 1 1/2 story, woodframe, white in color, destroyed prior to 1949.

The following information was extracted from the photographs and blueprint files of the Civil Engineering Branch, Engineering Division, First Coast Guard District, Boston, Massachusetts. A panoramic photograph of the station taken in 1892 shows from L North to South; a large barn, a house with an ell, a long shed, the light tower (unpainted) and the Fog Signal House. The house also shows on an original plan of the station, which unfortunately is undated.

By 1909, plans had been drafted to enlarge this house; later, photographs show the house was in fact altered to these plans. Modifications to the original dwelling were extensive; what had been a 34' x 26' one and one-half story duplex house was built over to form a 34 x 36 foot two and one-half story duplex. The enlarged house was destroyed prior to 1949, thus, eliminating all traces of the original house. The large barn was razed at about the same time.

Sometime before 1922, most probably in 1917, a second house was constructed, abutting the southerly end of the Rain Shed. In 1948, or 1949, this house was substantially altered by raising the roof and adding two upstairs bedrooms. It is this dwelling which exists today. The long shed mentioned above was a rain shed for water catchment, it survived until 1944.

Finally, of the light tower and Engine House: By 1944, the tower had been painted white and fitted with a new, enlarged entryway; and the Fog Signal House had been altered by removing the tall chimney used with the steam-operated fog signal. The fog signal is a dual EIG-300/02 with a range of five miles. The fourth order fixed lens has been replaced with a type DCB-224 uncorrected candlepower light of 32,000 KW with an operational range of 25 miles.

Historical Significance:

Libby Island Light Station was ordered built by President James Monroe in 1822 and has never been rebuilt [sic]. According to old journals at the station there were thirty-five wrecks from 1856 to 1902, and out of this number only fifteen lives were lost owing to the efficient work and valor of the light keepers at the station.

Among the ships lost to the sea near the Libby Island Station were the Schooner *Caledonia* of Windsor, Nova Scotia. The captain and crew were swept overboard by the breakers but two passengers were rescued by the volunteer lifesaving crew from *Starboard* in 1878. The Bark Fame drifted shore on the point in a heavy gale; twelve of a crew of fifteen were rescued by the heroic keepers, who waded into the surf and threw a rope to the crew, then rigged a boatswain chair and got all but three ashore safely. In 1892 the ship *Princeport* was wrecked on the bar between the two islands. After a perilous trip from the light the keepers reached the small piece of the bow, all that remained of the ship, and rescued the crew. The Schooner *F.C. Lockhart* with all sails set, making a beautiful picture, struck the point where she lodged between a natural cradle of rocks where she had to be left until the sea claimed her.

The Barkentine *John N. Myers* met disaster on the southwest end of East Libby Island in 1925. The crew managed to make a small lonely island from which they were taken off by the Coast Guard the next morning. The last square rigger to go ashore at Libby Island was the Barkentine *Africa* in 1902.

In a vain effort to save the ship both anchors, weighing over 5000 pounds, were thrown overboard by the crew, which subsequently escaped to the Island by small boat. These anchors, the only remnants of a once proud ship exist today in an excellent state of preservation.

Additional Information

Libby Island Light is Maine's third oldest standing light station. Only Portland Head Light (1790) and Burnt

Island Light (1811) were operational prior to the current Libby Island Light.

The light marks the entrance to Machias Bay and also serves as a coastal light, much like Moose Peak Light.

In 1822, a rubblestone tower was built at the south end of Libby Island by local contractors, along with a wood-frame keeper's house. Unfortunately the tower soon developed a large crack and collapsed after only a few months in the Spring of 1823.

Lesson learned, a second tower was immediately constructed, made from granite blocks. This tower proved to be much more sturdy, evidenced by the fact that it still stands today, nearly two centuries later. The granite block construction bears a strong resemblance to the work of Alexander Parris, noted Boston architect who was responsible for several other granite block light towers in Maine.

In 1974, the Fresnel lens was removed and the lighthouse was automated with a modern optic. Most of the buildings except the lighthouse tower and fog signal building have been destroyed over the years.

Under the Maine Lights Program, the lighthouse was turned over to the U.S. Fish and Wildlife Service in 1998.

The Coast Guard completed an overhaul of the tower in the summer of 2000. As part of the restoration the tower was returned to its original, unpainted, granite surface.

Best Viewing

Libby Island Light is located on Libby Island near the entrance to Machias Bay, nearest to the town of

Machiasport. This lighthouse is not accessible to the public and is best seen by boat.

As with other coastal light stations along the Maine's northeastern coast, *Bar Harbor Whale Watch* offers a yearly "Grand Slam" 18-lighthouse tour that includes Libby Island Light. For more information: *https://www.barharborwhales.com*

***

61 Little River Light

Year Established: 1847
Nearest to: Cutler
Latitude: 44° 39' 03" N
Longitude: 67° 11' 31" W
Tower Height: 35ft
Elevation: 56ft
Design: Conical Tower
1st Designer(s): Unknown (1847)
2nd Designer(s): U.S. Army Corps of Engineers (1876)
Material: Cast Iron
Light Sequence: White light – 6 sec. on – repeating
Fog Horn: One blast every ten seconds

Source: U.S. Coast Guard

National Register of Historic Places (01/29/1988)

Physical Appearance:

The Little River Light Station is composed of a tapered cylindrical iron light tower, a detached two-story frame keeper's house, a boathouse, and an oil house. A skeleton tower at the rock ledge now carries the beacon placed here when the station was automated.

One of only a handful of iron light towers in Maine, this handsome example, which was erected in 1876, is constructed of four distinct sections supported by a steel and brick frame. The tower reaches a height of thirty-five feet from its base to the center of the octagonal lantern. A door is located in the tower's north face and a segmentally arched two-over-two double hung sash window is framed by a bracketed, gabled hood.

A small bullseye window is positioned below the wide overhang of the parapet. This deck is supported by handsome brackets with pendants and is framed by a railing with ornamental iron posts. The lantern has a typical late nineteenth century configuration with a paneled iron base and a polygonal roof surmounted by a spherical ventilator. A small addition has been made to the tower's southeast face.

The keeper's house at Little River is an L-shaped wooden frame building that rests on a stone foundation. It was built in 1888 to replace the original 1847 stone dwelling. Its front (north) elevation contains a shed roofed porch that shelters a door and flanking window openings (all window openings have been boarded shut at this station). Both gable ends contain a window on each story, one above the other. The short ell, which projects toward the tower, features a pair of openings on each level. A short shed roofed porch carries across the west elevation of this ell. Behind it is a second entrance.

Historical Significance:

Established in 1847 and substantially rebuilt in 1876 and 1888, the Little River Light Station is located on Little River Island at the mouth of the Little River. It was built here not only as a guide to the refuge at Cutler Harbor but also as a navigational aid between the lights at West Quoddy Head to the northeast, Libby Island to the southwest and the Canadian seacoast light at Machias Seal Island.

The small community of Cutler is focused on Cutler Harbor which opens out to the south. Known for its deep, ice free character and the high protective bluffs that surround it, the harbor provided an important natural resource for the development of the village. Incorporated in 1826, Cutler had a population of 820 persons in 1850. Local nineteenth century industries included fishing, ship building and a herring box manufactory.

Additional Information

Cutler Harbor is the final protected harbor on the coast of Maine before reaching the St. Croix River on the Canadian border. Since no other light station existed between Libby Island and West Quoddy Head, a light at Cutler Harbor was seen as necessary as it would not only assist vessels entering the harbor, but also provide a navigational aid to ships traveling along the Atlantic coast.

Congress appropriated $5,000 in March 1847 to build a conical, twenty-three-and-half-foot-tall stone tower with an attached keeper's house on sixteen-acre Little River Island at the entrance to the harbor.

In 1876, the stone lighthouse was rebuilt. The 41-foot cast-iron tower, lined with brick, still stands. This light tower bears a strong resemblance in shape and construction to Cape Neddick Light (aka Nubble Light,) constructed three years later in 1879.

The light station was deactivated in 1975, when its Fresnel lens was removed and replaced by a modern optic mounted on a skeletal tower nearby. By 1981, the Coast Guard planned to tear down the lighthouse and sell the island, but this action was tabled following the intervention of a prominent local resident.

However, without a resident keeper, the abandoned Little River Light soon fell into disrepair. Its condition deteriorated to the point where it was listed as one of Maine's *Ten Most Endangered Historic Properties* by the Maine Preservation Society.

Fortunately, in 2000, the Coast Guard enlisted the help of American Lighthouse Foundation. Since then, restoration work to the keeper's house and tower has been substantial. During the summer of 2000, the wooden walkway from the boathouse to the lighthouse was completely rebuilt by the Coast Guard, with financial help from the Foundation.

In 2001, the American Lighthouse Foundation restored the lantern room so that the Coast Guard could install a new beacon in the tower that had been dark for 26 years. During the relighting ceremony on October 2, 2001, the light tower was draped in a large flag and relit as the *Beacon of Freedom to the World* in remembrance of the 9/11 terrorist attacks which had occurred just a few weeks prior to the ceremony.

In 2002, Little River Light became the first lighthouse in New England, and the third in the United States, to be transferred under the National Historic Lighthouse Preservation Act of 2000. Ownership of the light station was officially transferred to the American Lighthouse Foundation during a transfer ceremony in Cutler on July 27, 2002.

Best Viewing

Little River Light is located on Little River Island in Curtis Harbor, nearest to the town of Cutler. The lighthouse is not visible from the mainland and is best viewed via boat cruises offered in the area, such as those offered by the *Bold Coast Charter Company*, based in Cutler: *https://boldcoast.com/*

The light station is manager by *Friends of Little River Lighthouse*, a chapter of the American Lighthouse Foundation. Overnight stays are available in the keeper's house. According to the Friends' website:

How do you get to this amazing place?

No worries...the volunteers of the Friends of Little River Lighthouse will meet you at the public boat ramp in Cutler and take you and your guests on a twelve minute boat ride to this one-of-a-kind paradise – a place where peaceful solitude reigns without disturbance and memories in the making are waiting to be embraced!

http://www.littleriverlight.org/

***

62 West Quoddy Head Light

Year Established: 1808
Nearest to: Lubec
Latitude: 44° 48' 54" N
Longitude: 66° 57' 02" W
Tower Height: 49ft
Elevation: 83ft
Design: Conical Tower

Source: National Archives

1st Designer(s): Benjamin Beal / Duncan W. Thaxter (1808)
2nd Designer(s): Joseph Berry (1837)
3rd Designer(s): Unknown (1857)
Material: Brick
Light Sequence: White light - 2 sec. on, 2 sec. off, 2 sec. on, 9 sec. off - repeating.
Fog Horn:

National Register of Historic Places (05/19/1980)

Physical Appearance:

West Quoddy Head Light Station, dating from 1808 and 1858, is an early and well-preserved example of the form in brick. Two principal structures are present, the lighthouse and the keeper's quarters. The lighthouse consists of a circular tower 49 feet tall above the ground and narrower at the top than at the base. Above this the light proper, with an 18-mile maximum range, rises 83 feet above the water. At the top of the tower is an iron railing and slightly projecting walkway, and there is a similar feature at the level of the light. The most distinctive aspect of the lighthouse tower are the alternating red and white horizontal bands. A covered brick entry and attached frame entry are both covered by gabled roofs.

The 1-story keeper's house is of frame construction with gabled roof, 3 brick chimneys, vinyl siding, and brick foundation. Fenestration is 6/6 throughout The six-bayed facade faces north and has an off-center entrance. Above this is a shed-roofed dormer containing two windows. At the rear of the house is an ell and attached shed with design and detail equivalent to that of the house. A hip roofed wood frame service building and a gabled roofed wood frame oil house complete the light station complex.

Historical Significance:

West Quoddy Head Light Station, first authorized in 1808 and rebuilt in 1858, is one of the earliest such installations on the Maine coast and the first east of Penobscot Bay. It is also distinguished as the easternmost light in the United States. In 1869 a steam operated horn was installed to replace the old fog bell. West Quoddy was one of the first two stations in the country to be so equipped.

Picturesquely sited with a magnificent view across Quoddy Roads to the palisades of Grand Manan Island, West Quoddy Head Light with its red and white stripes is an internationally known landmark and a favorite tourist attraction.

Additional Information

West Quoddy Head is a peninsula in southeastern Lubec, overlooking Quoddy Narrows. The Narrows provide a sea passage route to Passamaquoddy Bay, which shares its border with Maine and the Canadian Province of New Brunswick, and eventually leads to the St. Croix River.

In early 1807, Congress allocated $5,000 "to cause to be erected a light-house on West Passamaquoddy Head, at the entrance into the bay and harbor of Passamaquoddy, in the District of Maine.

A wooden lighthouse subsequently was built on the site in 1808, along with a small keepers dwelling, making it the first American lighthouse east of Penobscot Bay.

The wooden lighthouse was not well suited for the climate of downeast Maine, and a new 49 foot rubblestone lighthouse tower replaced the wooden tower in 1831.

The present 49-foot brick tower was erected in 1857. The new lighthouse received a third-order Fresnel lens. A Victorian keeper's house was built at the same time.

In order to make the tower more visible as a daymark, West Quoddy Head Light's distinctive red and white stripes were added soon after the present tower was built. Red stripes on lighthouses are common in Canada, where it helps them stand out against snow. The only other lighthouse in the United States with horizontal red and white strips is Assateague Light in Virginia.

In 1988, West Quoddy Head Light was automated, along with the Fort Point Light – making Owls Head Light the last remaining manned lighthouse in Maine.

Ownership of the light station was transferred to Maine's Bureau of Parks and Land under the Maine Lights Program in 1998. West Quoddy Lighthouse is still operational and continues to utilize the 1857 third-order Fresnel lens.

Best Viewing

This light is located on the most eastern point in the United States, in the Bay of Fundy, nearest the town of

Lubec. The lighthouse grounds are accessible via Quoddy Head Road at West Quoddy State Park, which has a visitors center as well as a museum in the keeper's house that is open during the summer season.

The *West Quoddy Head Light Keepers Association* operates a seasonal visitor center in the former keeper's house. For more information:

https://westquoddy.com/

West Quoddy Head Light is open to visitors one day per year on Maine Open Lighthouse Day. More information about this event can be found at:

http://www.lighthousefoundation.org/maine-open-lighthouse-day

63 Lubec Channel Light

Year Established: 1890
Nearest to: Lubec
Latitude: 44° 45' 31" N
Longitude: 66° 58' 35" W
Tower Height: 40ft
Elevation: 53ft
Design: Spark Plug

Source: National Archives

Designer(s): U.S. Army Corp of Engineers (1890)
Material: Cast Iron
Light Sequence: White light – 6 sec. on - repeating
Fog Horn: One blast every 15 seconds

National Register of Historic Places (01/29/1988)

Physical Appearance:

One of the three extant late nineteenth century "spark plug" lights, the 1890 Lubec Channel Light Station is composed of a wide round base clad in cast iron that supports a tapered three-stage tower. The base, which is of concrete construction embedded directly into the river channel, rises to a wide deck formerly covered by a roof. The deck is supported by a flared concave neck at the top of the tower base and is reached by attached iron ladders. Its iron railing has been removed. A door opens off of the deck into the interior quarters, and a trio of two-over-two double-hung sash windows punctuate the first level. A second pair of openings provides light to the second level and a row of bullseye windows are positioned below the bracketed walkway of the short third stage. This walkway is framed by a perimeter railing. The third stage of the tower is punctuated by a door and one small window.

An octagonal lantern with a spherical ventilator crowns the structure. A solar panel has been added to the gallery since the station's automation.

Historical Significance:

Erected in 1890, the Lubec Channel Light Station occupies a strategic navigational location in this broad but shallow waterway. It is one of three surviving "spark plug" lights in Maine.

An effort to establish a light station in the Lubec Channel was made following the completion of a dredging project. The 1883 Annual Report of the Light-House Board mentions the need for a light in order to make the channel of value to commerce at night. Throughout this period the river ports at Calais, Eastport and Lubec were thriving commercial centers much of whose livelihood was dependent upon navigation on the Saint Croix River and Lubec Channel. By 1888 Congress had appropriated a total of $52,000 for construction of the station. It was put into service on December 31, 1890, and automated in 1939.

Additional Information

Similar to Goose Rock Light, Lubec Channel Light consists of a light tower built upon a submerged concrete-filled caisson. Unlike Goose Rocks Light, whose caisson was set upon bedrock, Lubec Channel Light required a series of pilings to be driven into the mud sea floor to provide stability for the tower.

This subfoundation consists of 185 spruce piles driven within the caisson. Twenty-three of the piles form a ring around the perimeter of the caisson and were driven to a depth of 69 feet. In addition, 162 interior piles were driven to a depth ranging from 35 to 45 feet. The caisson was sunk to a depth of six feet and leveled, and then filled with concrete.

The light was automated in 1939, with the installation of an acetylene gas system and a sun valve.

In 1989 the light was to be discontinued, but local residents mounted a "Save the Sparkplug" campaign. In 1992, a $700,000 renovation restored Lubec Channel Light to its best condition in decades. The renovation included the stabilization of the foundation, which had developed a tilt over the years. New plates were installed on the caisson and an additional 200 cubic yards of concrete was pumped in.

Twelve additional piles were also driven through the caisson into bedrock. One of these piles was said to be driven 149 feet. The lighthouse still has a six-degree list but is considered stable.

In 2006, the lighthouse was made available to a under the guidelines of the National Historic Lighthouse Preservation Act of 2000. There were no applicants, so in July 2007 Lubec Channel Light was auctioned and sold to a private citizen.

Best Viewing

This lighthouse is located in the Lubec Channel, nearest to the town of Lubec. This light is not accessible to the public but can be easily viewed from many points along South Lubec Road in Lubec.

***

64 Whitlocks Mill Light

Year Established: 1892
Nearest to: Calais
Latitude: 45° 09' 45" N
Longitude: 67° 13' 38" W
Tower Height: 25ft
Elevation: 32ft
Design: Conical Tower

Source: U.S. Coast Guard

Designer(s): U.S. Army Corps of Engineers (1892)
Material: Brick
Light Sequence: Green light - 6 sec. on, 6 sec. off - repeating.
Fog Horn: No fog signal

National Register of Historic Places (12/07/1987)

Physical Appearance:

Situated on the south bank of the St. Croix River, Whitlocks Mill Light Station consists of a detached conical brick tower, a two-story stuccoed, gambrel roofed keeper's house, as well as a brick oil house, a pyramidal bell house and a hip roofed shed. The entire complex was built in 1909.

The light tower rests on a granite base. Its brick shaft rises to a narrow iron walkway with railing that projects beyond the conical tower. Behind the railing is an octagonal lantern with a polygonal roof and spherical ventilator. A door is located in the west face of the brick shaft.

The L-shaped keeper's house, which faces the river, is composed of a projecting two-bay gambrel roofed east end and an enclosed porch carrying across the recessed wall of the ell. Four six-over-six windows, a pair on each story, occupy the north gambrel end along with two small attic windows. There is one pedimented dormer on the recessed ell and a pair on the two-bay east elevation.

The fenestration pattern in the south gambrel end is similar to the one on the facade.

Historical Significance:

Whitlocks Mill Light Station was established in 1909 as a guide to the upper St. Croix River and the harbor at Calais. It was the last station built in Maine.

During the nineteenth and early twentieth century the St. Croix River was a heavily trafficked waterway on which vessels of all types carried a variety of cargoes from commercial centers located along both the United States and Canadian sides of the river. The construction in 1856 on Dochet Island of the St. Croix River Light Station (destroyed) underscores the significance of the waterway.

Beginning in the 1820s Calais, situated just to the northwest of Whitlocks Mill light, developed into an important lumber shipping terminal. By the turn of the century the community contained a long and varied list of general merchants and manufacturers. Despite access to the Washington County Railroad much of the city's commerce continued to be dependent on maritime transportation.

Not until 1892, however, had the Light-House Board placed an aid to navigation at this site. The red lantern affixed to a tree was finally replaced by the present light station in 1909. The light has been automated and the ancillary buildings sold to a private citizen.

Additional Information

Whitlocks Mill Lighthouse has the dual distinction of being the last government-built and the northernmost of all lighthouses in Maine. The town of Calias also has the distinction of being situated exactly midway between the Equator and North Pole. By the 1860s, Calais' sawmills could process 55 million feet of timber per year. The town's port was navigable nine months per year and produced a diverse set of commodities incliding bricks, bedsteads, brooms, carriages, timber, plaster, and ships for consumers. Calais remains a center of regional commerce today.

In 1892, a red lantern was hung from a tree on the American side of the St. Croix River, near Calais, to serve local navigation. Colin Whitlock, a local mill owner, was hired by the government to tend the lantern's light.

The light was intended to mark a dangerous turn on the St Croix River, complementing two lights on the Canadian side of the river.

Following the light's automation and the removal of its Fresnel lens to the Maine Lighthouse Museum in Rockland in 1969, the station was leased to the Washington County Vocational Technical Institute in the 1970s. Under circumstances not entirely clear, the three-bedroom, keeper's house and other outbuildings later became privately owned and closed to the public.

The *St. Croix Historical Society* http://stcroixhistorical.com/ applied for and was awarded ownership of the light tower in 1997, as part of the Maine Lights Program. The Coast Guard continues to maintain the tower's flashing green light.

Best Viewing

Whitlock's Mill Light is located on the south side of St. Croix River, nearest to the town of St. Croix. The lighthouse can be viewed from the *St. Croix River View Rest Area* on Route 1 in Calais. The rest area is announced by a "*Rest Area 1,500 ft*" sign from the south. Note that the lighthouse view may be somewhat obscured by trees in summer.

Although the lighthouse grounds are not open to the public, according the St Croix Historical Society, Whitlocks Mill Light may be visited with advance notice:

"the private owners have agreed that with advance coordination, small groups may visit it. The private owners graciously assist with maintenance of the light house and its bell tower."

65 Ladies Delight Light

Year Established: 1908
Nearest to: Winthrop
Latitude: 44° 30' 44" N
Longitude: 69° 89' 66" W
Tower Height: 25ft
Elevation: Unknown
Design: Conical Tower
Designer(s): Frank Morse (1908)
Material: Granite Block
Light Sequence:
Fog Horn: No fog signal

Source: National Historic Register

National Register of Historic Places (11/29/1983)

Physical Appearance:

The Cobbossee Lighthouse, located on a tiny island near the north end of Lake Cobbosseecontee, is approximately 20 feet tall with a tapered cylindrical tower of rubblestone approximately eight feet in diameter at the base.

At the top of the tower is a very broad flat platform with a rail on which rests the hexagonal lantern. This in turn is capped with a flat conical roof with a vent at the peak. A plain door appears at the base of the tower to the left of which is a dedicatory plate. Above the door just under the platform appears a single glazed window with a counterpart on the opposite side.

Historical Significance:

The Cobbossee lighthouse was at the time of its construction in 1908, the only lighthouse on an inland lake east of the Mississippi and today it is still the only one in Maine with her hundreds of lakes. Although partly decorative, it has served its purpose as a navigational aid at night.

The lighthouse was built with funds donated by Daniel Robinson, the first commodore of the Cobbosseecontee Yacht Club which is the owner. At the time of its construction there were many hotels and restaurants on the lake and boats were used to transport people and on tours of the lake. When first built it was lit by two kerosene lamps which had to be tended every day.

Later storage batteries lasting 13 days powered an electric lamp and today an underwater cable serves a revolving light. The light is, of course, extinguished in winter when the lake is frozen over. The island on which it is located is properly named Ladies Delight, not Packards Ledge as indicated on the Geological Survey quadrangle.

Additional Information

Lake Cobbosseecontee, located near Augusta, is nearly nine miles long and has an average width of one mile. The lake's name is believed to be an Abenaki word that means "the place of many sturgeon."

As steamers circled the lake making various stops along the way, one such stop was a small rocky reef where the ladies could make a comfort visit. According to local legend, this is how the small islet became known as "Ladies Delight."

While Ladies Delight may have been a relief to some, it posed a serious threat to mariners, especially at night. In response, the Cobbosseecontee Yacht Club hired Frank Morse, a Boston architect, to design a lighthouse to mark Ladies Delight, and in 1908, the yacht club erected the sixteen-foot-tall granite lighthouse, making it the only landlocked lighthouse in the State of Maine.

Kerosene lanterns served as the tower's original light source, with a volunteer from the yacht club visiting the island each evening to service the light. The lighthouse now receives power to its custom-made lamp from a submarine cable.

The Cobbosseecontee Yacht Club initiated a restoration of Ladies Delight Lighthouse in 2001. That year, a severe list that had developed in the tower was corrected.

A bronze plaque was installed on the tower in 2008, the hundredth anniversary of the lighthouse. The tower was power washed and refinished in 2011, leaving it gleaming white once again.

Best Viewing

Ladies Delight Light is located on Lake Cobbosseecontee in Winthrop. This light is maintained by Cobbosseecontee Yacht Club and is not accessible to the public; however it is easily viewed by boat.

***

The Evolution and Restoration of Maine's Lighthouses

During the 1700s, maritime shipping was brisk as people and goods travelled back and forth between Europe and America. In this era before railroads were constructed, maritime vessels were also the main means of transportation up and down the Atlantic coast.

In order to point mariners toward their destination ports, bonfires and torches were often lit and maintained by local residents who desperately needed supplies in order to survive. These eventually gave way to wooden towers and kerosene lamps placed at strategic points not only to call attention to their location, but also to warn vessels of area hazards.

The first lighthouse built in America was the Boston Light, constructed by the city in 1716. Soon after, lighthouses were dotting the coast from Delaware to North Carolina, where navigation was difficult and treacherous. Not until nearly 80 years later, in 1795, did the first lighthouse appear in Maine – Portland Head Point, ordered by newly appointed president George Washington, who understood the importance of developing a navigational system of lighthouses along the North Atlantic coast.

During the early days of the Federal Government, lighthouse appropriations fell under the responsibility of the U.S. Treasury Department, whose primary goal was to spend as little money as possible on the lights. As a result, construction bids were awarded to the lowest bidders, who were inexperienced in lighthouse construction methods, often using inferior material and techniques. Needless to say, these lighthouses often quickly fell into disrepair.

A significant change occurred in 1851, when Congress moved the responsibility for lighthouses from the Treasury's Lighthouse Establishment to the newly formed

United States Lighthouse Board, the second agency created by the US Federal Government and responsible for the construction and maintenance of all lighthouses and navigation aids in the United States.

The quasi-military Lighthouse Board first met on April 28, 1851, and with its establishment, the administration of lighthouses and other aids to navigation would take their largest leap toward modernization since the inception of federal government control.

The Lighthouse Board brought the most active period of lighthouse refitting and construction in the history of Maine. During the 25 year period of 1851-1875, 34 of Maine's 65 lighthouses were either newly constructed or completely rebuilt.

The Lighthouse Board also brought with it strict responsibilities for lighthouse keepers and standardization of lighthouse design. One example of this was the Fresnel lighthouse lens. For years, mariners had complained that the lighthouses of Europe were much brighter than those in America. After examination by the Lighthouse Board, by 1875, every government-owned lighthouse in America was fitted with a French-made Fresnel lens.

By 1910, as lighthouse construction waned, the Lighthouse Board was disestablished in favor of a more civilian Lighthouse Service, under the Department of Commerce; later the Lighthouse Service was merged into the United States Coast Guard in 1939. During this period, the primary focus was the operation and maintenance of existing lighthouses.

The Coast Guard had many other responsibilities, and was not necessarily overjoyed with their added lighthouse duties. They saw their role as modernizing maritime navigation, and making lighthouses more efficient, not in preserving them. During the period of 1930-1980, the Coast Guard automated all of Maine's lighthouses, razed many buildings, and began to auction, sell, and transfer light stations that it deemed were no longer necessary.

During one three-year period during the depression era, from 1933-1935, the Coast Guard sold 7 Maine Light Stations to private individuals. All of these stations, except one, remain in private hands today, with no public access.

By 1990, the Coast Guard had transferred the maintenance of 17 lighthouses, although it still maintained the active beacons, most of which had had their Fresnel lenses removed and were replaced by cheaper and more efficient modern optics.

At this time, another significant event occurred. The *Island Institute of Rockland* wished to preserve the light station at Heron Neck after a fire broke out, and eventually succeeded in gaining a lease to the station in 1994, but during the four years of negotiation with the Coast Guard, unnecessary deterioration had occurred between the time of the fire and the signing of an interim lease agreement.

Based on its experience, and worried that many of Maine's lighthouses would not be preserved, nor accessible to the public, the Institute proposed that a streamlined process be developed for transferring a large number of Maine lighthouses to deserving non-profits, educational institutions, or government entities.

The result was the creation of the *Maine Lights Program*, which, since 1996, has facilitated the transfer of 41 Maine lighthouses to custodians capable of preserving the structures for the benefit of the public. As of 2019, the Coast Guard retained ownership of only one lighthouse in Maine, the remote Saddleback Ledge Light.

The success of the Maine Lights Program later led to the creation of the National Historic Lighthouse Preservation Act of 2000, which, according to a 2013 report, has enabled the transfer of over 100 additional lighthouses around the country to deserving parties. The tables which follow contain a complete list of significant dates for all Maine lighthouses.

#	Name	First Built Date	Last Rebuilt Date	Transfer Date
1	Whaleback Lighthouse	1829	1872	2008
2	Boon Island Lighthouse	1811	1855	2014
3	Cape Neddick Lighthouse	1879	1879	1998
4	Goat Island Lighthouse	1833	1859	1998
5	Wood Island Lighthouse	1808	1858	2004
6	Cape Elizabeth Lighthouse	1828	1874	1959/2001
7	Portland Head Lighthouse	1790	Original	1990
8	Ram Island Ledge Lighthouse	1905	Original	2010
9	Spring Point Ledge Lighthouse	1897	Original	1998
10	Portland Breakwater Lighthouse	1855	1875	1985
11	Halfway Rock Lighthouse	1871	Original	2014
12	Seguin Island Lighthouse	1796	1855	1998
13	Pond Island Lighthouse	1821	1855	1998
14	Perkins Island Lighthouse	1898	Original	2000
15	Squirrel Point Lighthouse	1898	Original	1998
16	Doubling Point Range Lighthouse	1898	Original	1997
17	Doubling Point Lighthouse	1898	Original	1997
18	Hendricks Head Lighthouse	1829	1875	1991
19	Cuckolds Lighthouse	1907	Original	2006
20	Burnt Island Lighthouse	1821	Original	1998
21	Ram Island Lighthouse	1883	Original	1983
22	Pemaquid Point Lighthouse	1827	1835	1940
23	Monhegan Island Lighthouse	1824	1855	1985
24	Franklin Island Lighthouse	1807	1855	1999
25	Marshall Point Lighthouse	1832	1857	1998
26	Tenants Harbor Lighthouse	1858	Original	1933
27	Whitehead Lighthouse	1804	1852	1992
28	Two Bush Island Lighthouse	1897	Original	1998
29	Matinicus Rock Lighthouse	1827	1855	1998
30	Owls Head Lighthouse	1825	1852	2007
31	Rockland Harbor Breakwater Lighthouse	1827	Original	1989
32	Rockland Harbor Southwest Lighthouse	1987	Original	Private
33	Indian Island Lighthouse	1854	1875	1934

#	Name	First Built Date	Last Rebuilt Date	Transfer Date
34	Curtis Island Lighthouse	1835	1896	1972
35	Grindle (Grindel) Point Lighthouse	1851	1875	1935
36	Fort Point Lighthouse	1836	1857	1998
37	Dice Head Lighthouse	1829	Original	1956
38	Pumpkin Island Lighthouse	1855	Original	1934
39	Eagle Island Lighthouse	1839	Original	1998
40	Goose Rocks Lighthouse	1890	Original	2006
41	Browns Head Lighthouse	1832	1857	1998
42	Heron Neck Lighthouse	1854	Original	1993
43	Saddleback Ledge Lighthouse	1839	Original	No Xfer
44	Isle au Haute Lighthouse	1907	Original	1998
45	Deer Island Thorofare Lighthouse	1858	Original	1997
46	Blue Hill Bay Lighthouse	1857	Original	1934
47	Burnt Coat Harbor Lighthouse	1872	Original	1994
48	Bass Harbor Head Lighthouse	1858	Original	2017
49	Great Duck Island Lighthouse	1890	Original	1984
50	Mount Desert Rock Island Lighthouse	1830	1847	1998
51	Baker Island Lighthouse	1828	1855	2011
52	Bear Island Lighthouse	1839	1889	1987
53	Egg Rock Lighthouse	1875	Original	1998
54	Winter Harbor Lighthouse	1857	Original	1934
55	Prospect Harbor Lighthouse	1850	1891	2000
56	Petit Manan Lighthouse	1817	1855	1974
57	Narraguagus Lighthouse	1853	Original	1934
58	Nash Island Lighthouse	1838	1874	1997
59	Moose Peak Lighthouse	1826	Unconfirmed	2012
60	Libby Island Lighthouse	1822	1824	1998
61	Little River Lighthouse	1847	1888	2000
62	Lubec Channel Lighthouse	1890	Original	2007
63	West Quoddy Head Lighthouse	1808	1857	1998
64	Whitlocks Mill Lighthouse	1892	1910	1999
65	Ladies Delight Lighthouse	1908	Original	No Xfer

***

How Far Away Can You See a Lighthouse?

How far away a person can sight a lighthouse from shore is limited by the fact that the earth is round. The curvature of the earth will at some point make an object disappear, as it goes over the horizon.

This holds true for how far away a mariner can view a lighthouse from a ship. A person lying down at the edge of the ocean with their eyes at approximately water level can only see a little more than a mile (1.23 miles to be exact) before the curve of the earth hides the object being viewed from sight.

The good news is that the higher above water level the lighthouse is, or the eye of the viewer, the greater the distance at which the light can still be seen.

This is why lighthouses are generally tall towers, or if shorter, are built on cliffs or hills to raise them far above water level. The light in a 100 foot tall lighthouse will be seen much farther away than the light in a 50 foot lighthouse. This is also why ships use crow's nests to view objects across the sea.

An easy way to calculate how far away an item can be sighted from shore is to multiply the square root of the elevation above water level by 1.23 miles. For example: a person standing on a cliff with their eyes 100 feet above the water will be able to view a point 12.3 miles away (square root of 100 equals 10, 10 times 1.23 miles = 12.3 miles.) Conversely, a lighthouse sanding 100 feet above sea level would be visible from 12.3 miles away by a viewer viewing from sea level.

But, in the case of mariners, they are likely aboard a ship at a higher level above the water. A mariner standing aboard a ship 20 feet above the water, for example, and looking at that lighthouse tower 100 feet above the water would be able to see it at a distance of 17.8 miles. We can again use our formula to verify this: (square root of 100 = 10, 10 x 1.23 miles = 12.3 miles) plus (square root of 20 = 4.5, 4.5 x 1.23 miles = 5.5 miles) for a total viewable range of 12.3 miles + 5.5 miles, or 17.8 miles.

In a trick to extend the viewable distance of lighthouses even more, lighthouse lenses take advantage of a principal known as *refraction*, or the bending of light rays. Refraction was an important innovation of the design of the Fresnel lens, as we will learn in the next chapter.

Using the light refraction in a Fresnel lens, the horizon effectively moves back from 1.23 miles to 1.32 miles. This might seem like a small amount, but in the example above it increases the viewable distance from 17.8 miles to 19.1 miles! (square root of 100 = 10, 10 x 1.32 miles = 13.2 miles) plus (square root of 20 = 4.5, 4.5 x 1.32 miles = 5.9 miles) for a total viewable range of 13.2 miles + 5.9 miles, or 19.1 miles.

Whether the light is of low intensity, or very bright, the same principles of elevation and refraction apply. However, of course, a brighter light is *easier* to see at longer distances than a weaker light. This is why tall offshore lighthouses, which are intended to be seen at great distance, have the largest and most powerful Fresnel lenses. Otherwise, a light that theoretically could be seen from a distance of 19 miles might fade from view in a far lesser distance due to conditions such as fog, haze, dust, smoke, or precipitation.

Colored lights, or colored panels in the lenses, especially green ones, also significantly reduce the distance at which a light could be seen. This is why offshore lights are nearly always white lights.

The tables which follow contain a complete list of lighthouse elevations and current visible range for all Maine lighthouses, sorted from most visible to least visible.

Wherever possible, the visible ranges are those published in the Coast Guard's most recent "Light List," which takes into account lighthouse elevation, light refraction, light intensity, and light color. As explained in the Coast Guard document:

"The nominal range given in this Light List is the maximum distance a given light can be seen when the meteorological visibility is 10 nautical miles. If the existing visibility is less than 10 NM, the range at which the light can be seen will be reduced below its nominal range. And, if the visibility is greater than 10 NM, the light can be seen at greater distances. The distance at which a light may be expected to be seen in the prevailing visibility is called its luminous range."

#	Name	Tower Height	Tower Elevation (Above Mean Sea Level)	Visable Range
7	Portland Head Lighthouse	80 ft	104 ft	24 nm
28	Two Bush Island Lighthouse	42 ft	65 ft	21 nm
23	Monhegan Island Lighthouse	47 ft	178 ft	20 nm
29	Matinicus Rock Lighthouse	53 ft	90 ft	20 nm
50	Mount Desert Rock Island Lighthouse	58 ft	75 ft	20 nm
59	Moose Peak Lighthouse	57 ft	72 ft	20 nm
11	Halfway Rock Lighthouse	76 ft	77 ft	19 nm
49	Great Duck Island Lighthouse	36 ft	67 ft	19 nm
56	Petit Manan Lighthouse	119 ft	123 ft	19 nm
12	Seguin Island Lighthouse	53 ft	180 ft	18 nm
53	Egg Rock Lighthouse	40 ft	64 ft	18 nm
60	Libby Island Lighthouse	42 ft	91 ft	18 nm
63	West Quoddy Head Lighthouse	49 ft	83 ft	18 nm
31	Rockland Harbor Breakwater Lighthouse	25 ft	38 ft	17 nm
30	Owls Head Lighthouse	30 ft	100 ft	16 nm
6	Cape Elizabeth Lighthouse	65 ft	129 ft	15 nm
36	Fort Point Lighthouse	31 ft	88 ft	15 nm
2	Boon Island Lighthouse	133 ft	137 ft	14 nm
22	Pemaquid Point Lighthouse	34 ft	79 ft	14 nm
41	Browns Head Lighthouse	18 ft	39 ft	14 nm
61	Little River Lighthouse	41 ft	56 ft	14 nm
3	Cape Neddick Lighthouse	41 ft	88 ft	13 nm
5	Wood Island Lighthouse	47 ft	71 ft	13 nm
25	Marshall Point Lighthouse	31 ft	30 ft	13 nm
48	Bass Harbor Head Lighthouse	32 ft	56 ft	13 nm
4	Goat Island Lighthouse	25 ft	38 ft	12 nm
9	Spring Point Ledge Lighthouse	25 ft	54 ft	12 nm
19	Cuckolds Lighthouse	48 ft	59 ft	12 nm
32	Rockland Harbor Southwest Lighthouse	44 ft.	44 ft	12 nm
40	Goose Rocks Lighthouse	51 ft	51 ft	12 nm
1	Whaleback Lighthouse	70 ft	59 ft	11 nm
21	Ram Island Lighthouse	49 ft	36 ft	11 nm
37	Dice Head Lighthouse	51 ft	134 ft	11 nm

The Complete Guide to Maine's Lighthouses

#	Name	Tower Height	Tower Elevation (Above Mean Sea Level)	Visable Range
51	Baker Island Lighthouse	45 ft	105 ft	10 nm
8	Ram Island Ledge Lighthouse	72 ft	78 ft	9 nm
13	Pond Island Lighthouse	20 ft	52 ft	9 nm
15	Squirrel Point Lighthouse	25 ft	33 ft	9 nm
16	Doubling Point Range Lighthouse	17 ft	33 ft	9 nm
17	Doubling Point Lighthouse	23 fr	23 ft	9 nm
18	Hendricks Head Lighthouse	39 ft	43 ft	9 nm
39	Eagle Island Lighthouse	30 ft	106 ft	9 nm
42	Heron Neck Lighthouse	30 ft	92 ft	9 nm
43	Saddleback Ledge Lighthouse	43 ft	52 ft	9 nm
47	Burnt Coat Harbor Lighthouse	32 ft	75 ft	9 nm
55	Prospect Harbor Lighthouse	38 ft	42 ft	9 nm
20	Burnt Island Lighthouse	30 ft	61 ft	8 nm
24	Franklin Island Lighthouse	45 ft	57 ft	8 nm
44	Isle au Haute Lighthouse	40 ft	48 ft	8 nm
45	Deer Island Thorofare Lighthouse	25 ft	52 ft	8 nm
10	Portland Breakwater Lighthouse	26 ft	30 ft	6 nm
14	Perkins Island Lighthouse	23 ft	41 ft	6 nm
27	Whitehead Lighthouse	41 ft	75 ft	6 nm
34	Curtis Island Lighthouse	25 ft	52 ft	6 nm
62	Lubec Channel Lighthouse	40 ft	53 ft	6 nm
46	Blue Hill Bay Lighthouse	22 ft	28 ft	5 nm
64	Whitlocks Mill Lighthouse	25 ft	32 ft	5 nm
35	Grindle (Grindel) Point Lighthouse	39 ft	39 ft	4 nm
52	Bear Island Lighthouse	31 ft	100 ft	4 nm
26	Tenants Harbor Lighthouse	27 ft	69 ft	None
33	Indian Island Lighthouse	37 ft	53 ft	None
38	Pumpkin Island Lighthouse	28 ft	43 ft	None
54	Winter Harbor Lighthouse	19 ft	37 ft	None
57	Narraguagus Lighthouse	31 ft	54 ft	None
58	Nash Island Lighthouse	29 ft	51 ft	None
65	Ladies Delight Lighthouse	25 ft	Unknown	Unknown

***

What's in a Light?

After the establishment of the Lighthouse Board in 1852, all lighthouses in the United States were eventually upgraded with the most widely regarded beacon in the world – the Fresnel lens.

Augustin-Jean Fresnel is the man behind the Fresnel lens. The first Fresnel lens was installed in a lighthouse in southwest France in 1823. That light was reported to have a visible range of 20 miles, exceeding the range of any other lighthouse beacon of its day by *a factor of four*.

Fresnel had invented a thinner, lighter beacon by making by molding glass into a series of concentric steps with an angular progression which resulted in a very strong beam of light.

The basic concept of a Fresnel lens can be explained as follows. Imagine taking a round magnifying glass lens and slicing it into ten concentric rings, like the growth rings of a tree. Now take each of the ten rings, and push them out from the edge to the center, making a cone-shaped lens. Now, picture that as you push the rings out to make the cone, the edge of each ring forms a progressive angle that continually aims light from each ring towards the point of the cone at the center of the glass. With this, you have created the basics of a Fresnel lens.

From this simple principle of concentric, angled rings, many enhancements were added that made the Fresnel lens the most efficient lighthouse lens in the world for over 100 years. Fresnel's work eventually evolved into six styles, or orders, of lenses. The first-order Fresnel lens was the largest, at over 8 feet tall, the most expensive, and most powerful of all the Fresnel lenses.

The first-order Fresnel was followed in succession to the smallest sixth-order Fresnel lens, at a little over one foot tall, as pictured below:

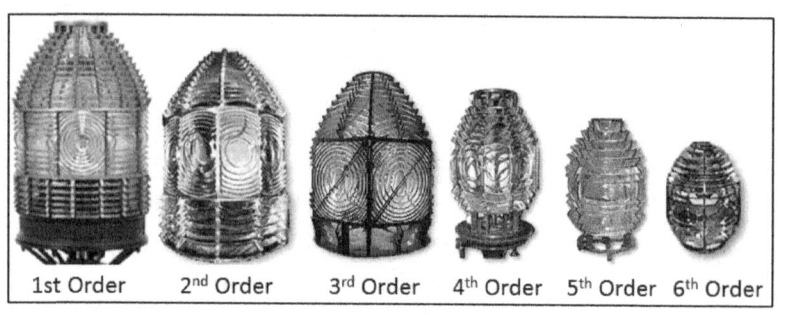

| 1st Order | 2nd Order | 3rd Order | 4th Order | 5th Order | 6th Order |

Source: www.partsolutions.com

Ten of Maine's lighthouses still operate today with an original Fresnel lens, including the only first-order Fresnel ever installed in Maine at Seguin Island Light. These lights are maintained for their historic value and as a tribute to the thousands of mariners who were guided safely by Fresnel's invention.

In Rockland, the Maine Lighthouse Museum houses the country's largest collection of Fresnel lenses. For an up-close look at their design and history, this is a must-see: *http://www.mainelighthousemuseum.com/*.

Maine's remaining operating lighthouses utilize modern optics, particularly the VLB-25 (18 lighthouses) and the VRB-44 (12 lighthouses.)

The VRB-25 is a lighthouse optical system designed and built by Vega Industries in New Zealand. It was originally designed in the 1990s with the assistance of the United States Coast Guard to meet requirements for a robust mechanism requiring minimum maintenance. During the late 1990s and early 2000s, it became the Coast Guard's standard 12 volt rotating beacon, with more than 400 installations worldwide.

The new VLB-44 LED beacon, also manufactured by Vega Industries of New Zealand, is completely self-contained, requires nearly no maintenance, has a life span of ten years and is just as bright – if not brighter than its predecessor, the VRB-25. As many of Maine's light stations convert to solar power, this low-power LED-based beacon is becoming the new Coast Guard standard.

The following tables list the former and current beacons used at each Maine lighthouse, sorted by the original Fresnel lenses they employed.

#	Name	Original Lens	Current Lens
12	Seguin Island Lighthouse	1st order Fresnel	1st order Fresnel
2	Boon Island Lighthouse	2nd order Fresnel	VRB-25
7	Portland Head Lighthouse	2nd order Fresnel	DCB-224
23	Monhegan Island Lighthouse	2nd order Fresnel	VRB-25
56	Petit Manan Lighthouse	2nd order Fresnel	VRB-25
59	Moose Peak Lighthouse	2nd order Fresnel	DCB-24
8	Ram Island Ledge Lighthouse	3rd order Fresnel	3rd order Fresnel
11	Halfway Rock Lighthouse	3rd order Fresnel	VRB-25
27	Whitehead Lighthouse	3rd order Fresnel	VLB-44
29	Matinicus Rock Lighthouse	3rd order Fresnel	VRB-25
50	Mount Desert Rock Island Lighthouse	3rd order Fresnel	VLB-44
63	West Quoddy Head Lighthouse	3rd order Fresnel	3rd order Fresnel
1	Whaleback Lighthouse	4th order Fresnel	VLB-44
3	Cape Neddick Lighthouse	4th order Fresnel	4th order Fresnel
5	Wood Island Lighthouse	4th order Fresnel	VLB-44
6	Cape Elizabeth Lighthouse	4th order Fresnel	VRB-25
19	Cuckolds Lighthouse	4th order Fresnel	VRB-25
20	Burnt Island Lighthouse	4th order Fresnel	300mm
21	Ram Island Lighthouse	4th order Fresnel	250mm
22	Pemaquid Point Lighthouse	4th order Fresnel	4th order Fresnel
24	Franklin Island Lighthouse	4th order Fresnel	VLB-44
26	Tenants Harbor Lighthouse	4th order Fresnel	No Light
30	Owls Head Lighthouse	4th order Fresnel	4th order Fresnel
31	Rockland Harbor Breakwater Lighthouse	4th order Fresnel	VRB-25
33	Indian Island Lighthouse	4th order Fresnel	No Light
34	Curtis Island Lighthouse	4th order Fresnel	VLB-44
36	Fort Point Lighthouse	4th order Fresnel	4th order Fresnel
37	Dice Head Lighthouse	4th order Fresnel	250mm
39	Eagle Island Lighthouse	4th order Fresnel	VLB-44
40	Goose Rocks Lighthouse	4th order Fresnel	250mm
45	Deer Island Thorofare Lighthouse	4th order Fresnel	VLB-44
46	Blue Hill Bay Lighthouse	4th order Fresnel	No Light
47	Burnt Coat Harbor Lighthouse	4th order Fresnel	VLB-44

The Complete Guide to Maine's Lighthouses

#	Name	Original Lens	Current Lens
49	Great Duck Island Lighthouse	4th order Fresnel	VRB-25
51	Baker Island Lighthouse	4th order Fresnel	VLB-44
58	Nash Island Lighthouse	4th order Fresnel	No Light
60	Libby Island Lighthouse	4th order Fresnel	VRB-25
64	Whitlocks Mill Lighthouse	4th order Fresnel	VLB-44
4	Goat Island Lighthouse	5th order Fresnel	VLB-44
9	Spring Point Ledge Lighthouse	5th order Fresnel	300mm Lexan
13	Pond Island Lighthouse	5th order Fresnel	250mm
14	Perkins Island Lighthouse	5th order Fresnel	250mm
15	Squirrel Point Lighthouse	5th order Fresnel	250mm
16	Doubling Point Range Lighthouse	5th order Fresnel	250mm
17	Doubling Point Lighthouse	5th order Fresnel	VLB-44
18	Hendricks Head Lighthouse	5th order Fresnel	250mm
25	Marshall Point Lighthouse	5th order Fresnel	VLB-44
28	Two Bush Island Lighthouse	5th order Fresnel	VRB-25
32	Rockland Harbor Southwest Lighthouse	5th order Fresnel	5th order Fresnel
35	Grindle (Grindel) Point Lighthouse	5th order Fresnel	VLB-44
38	Pumpkin Island Lighthouse	5th order Fresnel	No Light
41	Browns Head Lighthouse	5th order Fresnel	4th order Fresnel
42	Heron Neck Lighthouse	5th order Fresnel	300mm
43	Saddleback Ledge Lighthouse	5th order Fresnel	VLB-44
44	Isle au Haute Lighthouse	5th order Fresnel	250mm
48	Bass Harbor Head Lighthouse	5th order Fresnel	4th order Fresnel
52	Bear Island Lighthouse	5th order Fresnel	Acrylic
53	Egg Rock Lighthouse	5th order Fresnel	VRB-25
54	Winter Harbor Lighthouse	5th order Fresnel	No Light
55	Prospect Harbor Lighthouse	5th order Fresnel	250mm
57	Narraguagus Lighthouse	5th order Fresnel	No Light
61	Little River Lighthouse	5th order Fresnel	VLB-44
62	Lubec Channel Lighthouse	5th order Fresnel	VLB-44
10	Portland Breakwater Lighthouse	6th order Fresnel	250mm
65	Ladies Delight Lighthouse	Kerosene	Handmade

***

Maine Lighthouse Museums and Events

Maine Open Lighthouse Day

From 2015-2018, Maine Open Lighthouse Day has been sponsored by the Coast Guard, the State of Maine, and the American Lighthouse Foundation. Based on the success of this event, it is expected to continue into 2019 and beyond. Information for this event is available from the *American Lighthouse Foundation*:

http://www.lighthousefoundation.org/maine-open-lighthouse-day/

In 2018, 22 Maine lighthouses took part in this event, which offers the general public the rare opportunity to climb and learn about these historic Maine lights. The table below lists the currently participating lighthouses:

#	Name	First Built	Last Rebuilt	Location	Tower Shape	Tower Material
4	Goat Island Lighthouse	1833	1859	Cape Porpoise	Cylindrical	Brick
5	Wood Island Lighthouse	1808	1858	Biddeford	Conical	Granite Block
7	Portland Head Lighthouse	1790	1790	Cape Elizabeth	Conical	Rubblestone/Brick
9	Spring Point Ledge Lighthouse	1897	1897	South Portland	Spark Plug	Cast Iron/Brick
10	Portland Breakwater Lighthouse	1855	1875	South Portland	Cylindrical	Cast Iron
12	Seguin Island Lighthouse	1796	1855	Georgetown	Conical	Granite Block
15	Squirrel Point Lighthouse	1898	1898	Arrowsic	Octagonal	Wood
16	Doubling Point Range Lighthouse	1898	1898	Arrowsic	Octagonal	Wood
17	Doubling Point Lighthouse	1898	1898	Arrowsic	Octagonal	Wood
20	Burnt Island Lighthouse	1821	1821	Southport	Conical	Rubblestone/Brick
22	Pemaquid Point Lighthouse	1827	1835	Bristol	Conical	Rubblestone
23	Monhegan Island Lighthouse	1824	1855	Monhegan	Conical	Granite Block
25	Marshall Point Lighthouse	1832	1857	St George	Cylindrical	Granite Block/Brick
27	Whitehead Lighthouse	1804	1852	St George	Conical	Granite Block
30	Owls Head Lighthouse	1825	1852	Owls Head	Cylindrical	Brick
34	Curtis Island Lighthouse	1835	1896	Camden	Cylindrical	Brick
35	Grindle (Grindel) Point Lighthouse	1851	1875	Ilsesboro	Square Taper	Brick
36	Fort Point Lighthouse	1836	1857	Stockton Springs	Square	Brick
37	Dice Head Lighthouse	1829	1829	Castine	Conical	Granite Rubble
47	Burnt Coat Harbor Lighthouse	1872	1872	Swans Island	Square	Brick
48	Bass Harbor Head Lighthouse	1858	1858	Bass Harbor	Cylindrical	Brick
63	West Quoddy Head Lighthouse	1808	1857	Lubec	Conical	Brick

The Maine Lighthouse Museum

The Maine Lighthouse Museum in Rockland boasts one of the United States' largest collections of Fresnel Lighthouse lenses. In 2007, the American Lighthouse Foundation merged the collection of the Museum of Lighthouse History in Wells with the Maine Lighthouse Museum, creating one of the largest lighthouse museums in the country. For more information: *https://www.mainelighthousemuseum.org/*

Resident Lighthouse Museums

For those seeking an in-depth experience, consider visiting one of the six lighthouses in Maine that house a resident museum. These museums are open seasonally and are generally staffed by personnel with wide knowledge of historical information. The table below lists these lighthouses. For more information, refer to the specific lighthouse's Chapter within this book.

#	NRHP Date	Name	Last Rebuilt	Location	Museum Custodian
10	1/23/1973	Portland Breakwater Lighthouse	1875	South Portland	City of South Portland
22	2/22/1985	Pemaquid Point Lighthouse	1835	Bristol	Friends of Pemaquid Point Lighthouse
23	12/3/1979	Monhegan Island Lighthouse	1855	Monhegan	Monhegan Historical and Cultural Museum Assoc
25	12/7/1987	Marshall Point Lighthouse	1857	St George	Town of St George
35	2/12/1987	Grindle (Grindel) Point Lighthouse	1875	Ilsesboro	Town of Isleboro
63	5/19/1980	West Quoddy Head Lighthouse	1857	Lubec	Maine State Bureau of Parks and Land

Lighthouse Towns and Cities in Maine

As you would expect, Maine's lighthouses are spread widely along coastal regions. There are, however many towns with multiple lighthouses.

There are four towns that lie claim to three lighthouses:

- Arrowsic
- Cape Elizabeth
- Georgetown
- Vinalhaven

And nine towns with two lighthouses:

- Deer Isle
- Frenchboro
- Lubec
- Owls Head
- South Portland
- Southport
- St George
- Winter Harbor
- York

The following table lists each lighthouse, sorted by their nearest towns and cities.

#	Name	Location	Custodian	Status	Mainland View
58	Nash Island Lighthouse	Addison	Friends of Nash Island Light	Deactivated	No View
15	Squirrel Point Lighthouse	Arrowsic	Citizens for Squirrel Point	Active	Near
16	Doubling Point Range Lighthouse	Arrowsic	The Range Light Keepers	Active	Near
17	Doubling Point Lighthouse	Arrowsic	Friends of Doubling Point Light	Active	Near
48	Bass Harbor Head Lighthouse	Bass Harbor	National Park Service	Active	Near
5	Wood Island Lighthouse	Biddeford	Wood Island Lighthouse Society	Active	Distant
21	Ram Island Lighthouse	Boothbay Harbor	Ram Island Preservation Society	Active	Distant
22	Pemaquid Point Lighthouse	Bristol	Friends of Pemaquid Point Lighthouse	Active	Near
46	Blue Hill Bay Lighthouse	Brooklin	Private	Deactivated	Distant
64	Whitlocks Mill Lighthouse	Calais	St Criox Historical Society	Active	Moderate
34	Curtis Island Lighthouse	Camden	Town of Camden	Active	Moderate
6	Cape Elizabeth Lighthouse	Cape Elizabeth	American Lighthouse Foundation	Active (East)	Near
7	Portland Head Lighthouse	Cape Elizabeth	City of Cape Elizabeth	Active	Near
8	Ram Island Ledge Lighthouse	Cape Elizabeth	Private	Active	Distant
4	Goat Island Lighthouse	Cape Porpoise	Kennebunk Conservation Trust	Active	Distant
37	Dice Head Lighthouse	Castine	Town of Castine	Active	Near
56	Petit Manan Lighthouse	Corea	Maine Coastal Islands National Wildlife Refuge	Active	Distant
61	Little River Lighthouse	Cutler	Friends of Little River Lighthouse	Active	No View
38	Pumpkin Island Lighthouse	Deer Isle	Private	Deactivated	Moderate
39	Eagle Island Lighthouse	Deer Isle	Eagle Light Caretakers	Active	Distant
49	Great Duck Island Lighthouse	Frenchboro	College of the Atlantic	Active	No View
50	Mount Desert Rock Island Lighthouse	Frenchboro	College of the Atlantic	Active	No View
24	Franklin Island Lighthouse	Friendship	Franklin Light Preservation Inc.	Active	No View
12	Seguin Island Lighthouse	Georgetown	Friends of Seguin Island Light Station	Active	Distant
13	Pond Island Lighthouse	Georgetown	Maine Coastal Islands National Wildlife Refuge	Active	Distant
14	Perkins Island Lighthouse	Georgetown	American Lighthouse Foundation	Active	Distant
35	Grindle (Grindel) Point Lighthouse	Ilsesboro	Town of Islesboro	Active	Distant
44	Isle au Haute Lighthouse	Isle au Haute	Friends of the Isle au Haut Lighthouse	Active	No View
51	Baker Island Lighthouse	Isleboro	National Park Service	Active	No View
59	Moose Peak Lighthouse	Jonesport	Private	Active	No View
1	Whaleback Lighthouse	Kittery	Friends of Portsouth Harbor Lighthouses	Active	Moderate
63	West Quoddy Head Lighthouse	Lubec	Maine State Bureau of Parks and Land	Active	Near
62	Lubec Channel Lighthouse	Lubec	Private	Active	Moderate

The Complete Guide to Maine's Lighthouses

#	Name	Location	Custodian	Status	Mainland View
60	Libby Island Lighthouse	Machaisport	Maine Coastal Islands National Wildlife Refuge	Active	Distant
29	Matinicus Rock Lighthouse	Matinicus	Maine Coastal Islands National Wildlife Refuge	Active	No View
57	Narraguagus Lighthouse	Milbridge	Private	Deactivated	No View
23	Monhegan Island Lighthouse	Monhegan	Monhegan Historical and Cultural Museum Assoc	Active	No View
40	Goose Rocks Lighthouse	North Haven	Beacon Preservation Inc	Active	No View
52	Bear Island Lighthouse	Northeast Harbor	National Park Service	Private Aid	Distant
30	Owls Head Lighthouse	Owls Head	Friends of Rockland Harbor Lights	Active	Near
32	Rockland Harbor Southwest Lighthouse	Owls Head	Private	Private Aid	Near
11	Halfway Rock Lighthouse	Phippsburg,	Private	Active	Distant
55	Prospect Harbor Lighthouse	Prospect Harbor	American Lighthouse Foundation	Active	Moderate
33	Indian Island Lighthouse	Rockland	Private	Deactivated	Distant
31	Rockland Harbor Breakwater Lighthouse	Rockland Harbor	Friends of Rockland Harbor Lights	Active	Near
9	Spring Point Ledge Lighthouse	South Portland	Spring Point Ledge Light Trust	Active	Near
10	Portland Breakwater Lighthouse	South Portland	City of South Portland	Private Aid	Near
19	Cuckolds Lighthouse	Southport	Cuckholds Fog Signal and Light Station Council	Active	Distant
20	Burnt Island Lighthouse	Southport	Maine Dept of Marine Resources	Active	Moderate
28	Two Bush Island Lighthouse	Sprucehead	Maine Coastal Islands National Wildlife Refuge	Active	No View
25	Marshall Point Lighthouse	St George	Town of St George	Active	Near
27	Whitehead Lighthouse	St George	Pine Island Camp	Active	No View
36	Fort Point Lighthouse	Stockton Springs	Maine State Bureau of Parks and Land	Active	Near
45	Deer Island Thorofare Lighthouse	Stonington	Island Heritage Trust	Active	Distant
47	Burnt Coat Harbor Lighthouse	Swans Island	Friends of Swans Island Lighthouse	Active	No View
26	Tenants Harbor Lighthouse	Tenents Harbor	Private	Deactivated	No View
41	Browns Head Lighthouse	Vinalhaven	American Lighthouse Foundation	Active	No View
42	Heron Neck Lighthouse	Vinalhaven	Private	Active	No View
43	Saddleback Ledge Lighthouse	Vinalhaven	U.S. Coast Guard	Active	No View
18	Hendricks Head Lighthouse	West Southport	Private	Active	Moderate
53	Egg Rock Lighthouse	Winter Harbor	Maine Coastal Islands National Wildlife Refuge	Active	Distant
54	Winter Harbor Lighthouse	Winter Harbor	Private	Deactivated	Distant
65	Ladies Delight Lighthouse	Winthrop	Cobbosseecontee Yacht Club	Private Aid	Moderate
2	Boon Island Lighthouse	York	Private	Active	Distant
3	Cape Neddick Lighthouse	York	Town of York	Active	Near

***

The Complete Guide to Maine's Lighthouses

Maine Lighthouse Grounds Access

With a wide range of locations, owners and terrain, Maine's lighthouses have varying availability. Some are located in public parks, some on protected wildlife refuges, and others in the hands of private owners.

Fortunately, nearly half (29 to be exact) of Maine's lighthouse grounds are open to the public. The list that follows lists lighthouses that are available for up-close visits.

#	Name	Location	Custodian	Grounds Access
4	Goat Island Lighthouse	Cape Porpoise	Kennebunk Conservation Trust	Yes
5	Wood Island Lighthouse	Biddeford	Wood Island Lighthouse Society	Yes
7	Portland Head Lighthouse	Cape Elizabeth	City of Cape Elizabeth	Yes
9	Spring Point Ledge Lighthouse	South Portland	Spring Point Ledge Light Trust	Yes
10	Portland Breakwater Lighthouse	South Portland	City of South Portland	Yes
12	Seguin Island Lighthouse	Georgetown	Friends of Seguin Island Light Station	Yes
13	Pond Island Lighthouse	Georgetown	Maine Coastal Islands National Wildlife Refuge	Yes
14	Perkins Island Lighthouse	Georgetown	American Lighthouse Foundation	Yes
15	Squirrel Point Lighthouse	Arrowsic	Citizens for Squirrel Point	Yes
16	Doubling Point Range Lighthouse	Arrowsic	The Range Light Keepers	Yes
17	Doubling Point Lighthouse	Arrowsic	Friends of Doubling Point Light	Yes
19	Cuckolds Lighthouse	Southport	Cuckholds Fog Signal and Light Station Council	Yes
20	Burnt Island Lighthouse	Southport	Maine Dept of Marine Resources	Yes
22	Pemaquid Point Lighthouse	Bristol	Friends of Pemaquid Point Lighthouse	Yes
23	Monhegan Island Lighthouse	Monhegan	Monhegan Historical and Cultural Museum Assoc	Yes
25	Marshall Point Lighthouse	St George	Town of St George	Yes
31	Rockland Harbor Breakwater Lighthouse	Rockland Harbor	Friends of Rockland Harbor Lights	Yes
34	Curtis Island Lighthouse	Camden	Town of Camden	Yes
35	Grindle (Grindel) Point Lighthouse	Ilsesboro	Town of Islesboro	Yes
36	Fort Point Lighthouse	Stockton Springs	Maine State Bureau of Parks and Land	Yes
37	Dice Head Lighthouse	Castine	Town of Castine	Yes
41	Browns Head Lighthouse	Vinalhaven	American Lighthouse Foundation	Yes
44	Isle au Haute Lighthouse	Isle au Haute	Friends of the Isle au Haut Lighthouse	Yes
47	Burnt Coat Harbor Lighthouse	Swans Island	Friends of Swans Island Lighthouse	Yes
48	Bass Harbor Head Lighthouse	Bass Harbor	National Park Service	Yes
51	Baker Island Lighthouse	Islesboro	National Park Service	Yes
61	Little River Lighthouse	Cutler	Friends of Little River Lighthouse	Yes
63	West Quoddy Head Lighthouse	Lubec	Maine State Bureau of Parks and Land	Yes
64	Whitlocks Mill Lighthouse	Calais	St Croix Historical Society	Yes

***

Lighthouse Cruises Mentioned in this Book

While 22 of Maine's lighthouse are accessible from the mainland, 43 lighthouses are best viewed, or only viewed, by boat. The following list provides examples of boat cruises that claim to travel to, or past, these lights. The list is by no means inclusive – and it is always recommended that you check before assuming that a particular cruise will be available when you arrive.

1 Whaleback Light
Portsmouth Harbor Cruises
http://www.portsmouthharbor.com

2 Boon Island Light
Private charters
https://www.maine.gov/dmr/recreational-fishing/forhirefleet/yorkcounty.html

4 Goat Island Light
EcoAdventures
https://newenglandecoadventures.com/guided-tour-of-goat-island-light-house

8 Ram Island Ledge Light
Portland Discovery Land and Sea Tours
http://www.portlanddiscovery.com/tours/lighthouse-lovers-cruise

11 Halfway Rock Light
Casco Bay Adventures
www.cascobayadventures.com

12 Seguin Island Light
Maine Maritime Museum
https://www.mainemaritimemuseum.org/
Seguin Island Ferry
http://www.fishntripsmaine.com/seguinislandferry.html

13 Pond Island Light
Maine Maritime Museum
https://www.mainemaritimemuseum.org/

14 Perkins Island Light
Maine Maritime Museum
https://www.mainemaritimemuseum.org/

15 Squirrel Point Light
Maine Maritime Museum
https://www.mainemaritimemuseum.org/

16 Doubling Point Range Lights
Maine Maritime Museum
https://www.mainemaritimemuseum.org/

17 Doubling Point Light
Maine Maritime Museum
https://www.mainemaritimemuseum.org/

18 Hendricks Head Light
Maine Maritime Museum
https://www.mainemaritimemuseum.org/

19 Cuckolds Light
Cap'n Fish's Audubon Puffin & Scenic Cruises
https://www.mainepuffin.com/

20 Burnt Island Light
Maine Department of Marine Resources
https://www.maine.gov/dmr/education/burnt-island/tours.html

21 Ram Island Light
Maine Maritime Museum
https://www.mainemaritimemuseum.org/

23 Monhegan Island Light
Monhegan Boat Line
https://monheganboat.com/

24 Franklin Island Light
Midcoast Maine Lighthouse Challenge
http://www.lighthousefoundation.org/midcoast-lighthouse-challenge/

26 Tenants Harbor Light
Monhegan Boat Line
https://monheganboat.com

27 Whitehead Light
Monhegan Boat Line
https://monheganboat.com

28 Two Bush Island Light
Monhegan Boat Line
https://monheganboat.com

29 Matinicus Rock Light
Matinicus Excursions
http://www.matinicusexcursions.com/

33 Indian Island Light
Schooner *Heron*
https://sailheron.com/maine-schedule/

34 Curtis Island Light
Ducktrap Kayak
http://ducktrapkayak.com/
Breakwater Kayak
http://www.breakwaterkayak.com/

35 Grindle Point Light
Isleboro Ferry
https://www.maine.gov/mdot/ferry/islesboro/

39 Eagle Island Light
Mail Boat Katherine
https://www.eagleislandrentals.com/transportation

40 Goose Rocks Light
Old Quarry Ocean Adventures
https://www.oldquarry.com/

41 Browns Head Light
Vinalhaven Ferry
https://www.maine.gov/mdot/ferry/vinalhaven/

42 Heron Neck Light
Matinicus Excursions
http://www.matinicusexcursions.com/
Old Quarry Ocean Adventures
https://www.oldquarry.com/

43 Saddleback Ledge Light
Matinicus Excursions
http://www.matinicusexcursions.com/
Old Quarry Ocean Adventures
https://www.oldquarry.com/

44 Isle au Haut Light
Mail Boat/Passenger Ferry
http://isleauhautferryservice.com/

45 Deer Island Thorofare Light
Isle au Haut Company
http://isleauhautferryservice.com

46 Blue Hill Bay Light
Bar Harbor Whale Watch Co.
https://www.barharborwhales.com/

47 Burnt Coat Harbor Light
Swans Island Ferry
https://www.maine.gov/mdot/ferry/swansisland/

49 Great Duck Island Light
Bar Harbor Whale Watch Co.
https://www.barharborwhales.com/

51 Baker Island Light
Bar Harbor Whale Watch Co.
https://www.barharborwhales.com/

53 Egg Rock Light
Bar Harbor Whale Watch Co.
https://www.barharborwhales.com/

54 Winter Harbor Light
Bar Harbor Whale Watch Co.
https://www.barharborwhales.com/

56 Petit Manan Island Light
Acadian Boat Tours
https://acadianboattours.com/

57 Narraguagas Light
Robertson Sea Tours
http://www.robertsonseatours.com/lighthouse-tours/

58 Nash Island Light
Robertson Sea Tours
http://www.robertsonseatours.com/lighthouse-tours/

59 Moose Peak Island
Bar Harbor Whale Watch Co.
https://www.barharborwhales.com/

60 Libby Island Light
Bar Harbor Whale Watch Co.
https://www.barharborwhales.com/

61 Little River Light
Bold Coast Charter Company
https://boldcoast.com/

Mainland Lighthouse Views

In our final table, each Maine lighthouse is sorted according to whether the lighthouse can be viewed at near points, moderate points, distant points, or is not visible at all from the mainland.

As the table illustrates, 17 lighthouses can be viewed from near points i.e. lighthouse station grounds, 9 lighthouses can be viewed from moderate points i.e. across a small channel or river, 20 lighthouses can be viewed from distant points i.e. remote islands, and 19 lighthouses have no mainland viewing points at all.

#	Name	Location	Custodian	Mainland View
3	Cape Neddick Lighthouse	York	Town of York	Near
6	Cape Elizabeth Lighthouse	Cape Elizabeth	Private	Near
7	Portland Head Lighthouse	Cape Elizabeth	City of Cape Elizabeth	Near
9	Spring Point Ledge Lighthouse	South Portland	Spring Point Ledge Light Trust	Near
10	Portland Breakwater Lighthouse	South Portland	City of South Portland	Near
15	Squirrel Point Lighthouse	Arrowsic	Citizens for Squirrel Point	Near
16	Doubling Point Range Lighthouse	Arrowsic	The Range Light Keepers	Near
17	Doubling Point Lighthouse	Arrowsic	Friends of Doubling Point Light	Near
22	Pemaquid Point Lighthouse	Bristol	Friends of Pemaquid Point Lighthouse	Near
25	Marshall Point Lighthouse	St George	Town of St George	Near
30	Owls Head Lighthouse	Owls Head	Friends of Rockland Harbor Lights	Near
31	Rockland Harbor Breakwater Lighthouse	Rockland Harbor	Friends of Rockland Harbor Lights	Near
32	Rockland Harbor Southwest Lighthouse	Owls Head	Private	Near
36	Fort Point Lighthouse	Stockton Springs	Maine State Bureau of Parks and Land	Near
37	Dice Head Lighthouse	Castine	Town of Castine	Near
48	Bass Harbor Head Lighthouse	Bass Harbor	National Park Service	Near
63	West Quoddy Head Lighthouse	Lubec	Maine State Bureau of Parks and Land	Near
1	Whaleback Lighthouse	Kittery	Friends of Portsouth Harbor Lighthouses	Moderate
18	Hendricks Head Lighthouse	West Southport	Private	Moderate
20	Burnt Island Lighthouse	Southport	Maine Dept of Marine Resources	Moderate
34	Curtis Island Lighthouse	Camden	Town of Camden	Moderate
38	Pumpkin Island Lighthouse	Deer Isle	Private	Moderate
55	Prospect Harbor Lighthouse	Prospect Harbor	American Lighthouse Foundation	Moderate
62	Lubec Channel Lighthouse	Lubec	Private	Moderate
64	Whitlocks Mill Lighthouse	Calais	St Croix Historical Society	Moderate
65	Ladies Delight Lighthouse	Winthrop	Cobbosseecontee Yacht Club	Moderate
2	Boon Island Lighthouse	York	Private	Distant
4	Goat Island Lighthouse	Cape Porpoise	Kennebunk Conservation Trust	Distant
5	Wood Island Lighthouse	Biddeford	Wood Island Lighthouse Society	Distant
8	Ram Island Ledge Lighthouse	Cape Elizabeth	Private	Distant
11	Halfway Rock Lighthouse	Phippsburg,	Private	Distant
12	Seguin Island Lighthouse	Georgetown	Friends of Seguin Island Light Station	Distant
13	Pond Island Lighthouse	Georgetown	Maine Coastal Islands National Wildlife Refuge	Distant

The Complete Guide to Maine's Lighthouses

#	Name	Location	Custodian	Mainland View
14	Perkins Island Lighthouse	Georgetown	Friends of Perkins Island Lighthouse	Distant
19	Cuckolds Lighthouse	Southport	Cuckholds Fog Signal and Light Station Council	Distant
21	Ram Island Lighthouse	Boothbay Harbor	Ram Island Preservation Society	Distant
33	Indian Island Lighthouse	Rockland	Private	Distant
35	Grindle (Grindel) Point Lighthouse	Ilsesboro	Town of Isleboro	Distant
39	Eagle Island Lighthouse	Deer Isle	Eagle Light Caretakers	Distant
45	Deer Island Thorofare Lighthouse	Stonington	Island Heritiage Trust	Distant
46	Blue Hill Bay Lighthouse	Brooklin	Private	Distant
52	Bear Island Lighthouse	Northeast Harbor	National Park Service	Distant
53	Egg Rock Lighthouse	Winter Harbor	Maine Coastal Islands National Wildlife Refuge	Distant
54	Winter Harbor Lighthouse	Winter Harbor	Private	Distant
56	Petit Manan Lighthouse	Corea	Maine Coastal Islands National Wildlife Refuge	Distant
60	Libby Island Lighthouse	Machaisport	Maine Coastal Islands National Wildlife Refuge	Distant
23	Monhegan Island Lighthouse	Monhegan	Monhegan Historical and Cultural Museum Assoc	No View
24	Franklin Island Lighthouse	Friendship	Franklin Light Preservation Inc.	No View
26	Tenants Harbor Lighthouse	Tenents Harbor	Private	No View
27	Whitehead Lighthouse	St George	Pine Island Camp	No View
28	Two Bush Island Lighthouse	Sprucehead	Maine Coastal Islands National Wildlife Refuge	No View
29	Matinicus Rock Lighthouse	Matinicus	Maine Coastal Islands National Wildlife Refuge	No View
40	Goose Rocks Lighthouse	North Haven	Beacon Preservation Inc	No View
41	Browns Head Lighthouse	Vinalhaven	American Lighthouse Foundation	No View
42	Heron Neck Lighthouse	Vinalhaven	Private	No View
43	Saddleback Ledge Lighthouse	Vinalhaven	U.S. Coast Guard	No View
44	Isle au Haute Lighthouse	Isle au Haute	Friends of the Isle au Haut Lighthouse	No View
47	Burnt Coat Harbor Lighthouse	Swans Island	Friends of Swans Island Lighthouse	No View
49	Great Duck Island Lighthouse	Frenchboro	College of the Atlantic	No View
50	Mount Desert Rock Island Lighthouse	Frenchboro	College of the Atlantic	No View
51	Baker Island Lighthouse	Isleboro	National Park Service	No View
57	Narraguagus Lighthouse	Milbridge	Private	No View
58	Nash Island Lighthouse	Addison	Friends of Nash Island Light	No View
59	Moose Peak Lighthouse	Jonesport	Private	No View
61	Little River Lighthouse	Cutler	Friends of Little River Lighthouse	No View

***

Made in the USA
Middletown, DE
25 June 2019